NAPOLEONIC WARS
IN
CARTOONS

Also by Mark Bryant

Dictionary of British Cartoonists and
Caricaturists, 1730-1980 (with S. Heneage)

Dictionary of Twentieth-Century
British Cartoonists and Caricaturists

World War I in Cartoons

World War II in Cartoons

Wars of Empire in Cartoons

God in Cartoons

The Complete Colonel Blimp (ed.)

The Comic Cruikshank (ed.)

Vicky's Supermac (ed.)

Nicolas Bentley (ed.)

A. M. Bateman (ed.)

NAPOLEONIC WARS
IN
CARTOONS

Mark Bryant

GRUB STREET • LONDON

For Robert and Julius

First published 2009 by
Grub Street Publishing
4 Rainham Close, London, SW11 6SS

Copyright © Mark Bryant 2009

British Library Cataloguing in Publication Data

Bryant, Mark, 1953-
    The Napoleonic Wars in cartoons
    1. Napoleonic Wars, 1800-1815 – Art and the war
    2. Napoleonic Wars, 1800-1815 – Caricatures and cartoons
    I. Title
    940.2'7'0207

 ISBN: 978 1 906502 27 0

Design by Roy Platten, Eclipse
roy.eclipse@btopenworld.com

Printed in India by Replika Press

CONTENTS

PREFACE

THIS BOOK TAKES a similar approach to its companion volumes, *Wars of Empire in Cartoons*, *World War I in Cartoons* and *World War II in Cartoons*, in that it is intended primarily as a pictorial history of the period as seen through the eyes of the cartoonists and caricaturists who lived through it and chronicled the events as they occurred. In this case the period is the Napoleonic Wars but with an additional introductory chapter on the French Revolutionary Wars before Napoleon came to power. As with the earlier books, I have added some historical background to link the images and help put them in context and, where possible, I have also supplied some information about the artists themselves and the printsellers who originally published the images. In addition, I have once again tried to include material from both sides of the conflict but, as before, this has been limited somewhat by considerations of time and cost. The main emphasis has been on political and joke cartoons published as individual prints (the chief outlet for cartoons and caricature during this period) though material from other sources, such as books and early satirical magazines, has also been included.

In the preparation of this book I am indebted to Nick Hiley and Jane Newton of the British Cartoon Archive at the University of Kent, the British Library, the British Museum Department of Prints & Drawings, the Victoria & Albert Museum Department of Prints & Drawings, the Senate House Library of the University of London and the London Library. Last, but by no means least, my thanks also go to John Davies, Anne Dolamore, Hannah Stuart and all at Grub Street Publishing for all their support, and to the designer Roy Platten for producing such a handsome book.

Mark Bryant
London, 2009

INTRODUCTION

TWO CENTURIES have passed since the defeat of Napoleon at the Battle of Waterloo, marking the end of a long international struggle which inspired some of the greatest works of modern literature, notably Tolstoy's monumental classic, *War and Peace*. In more recent years it has also been the setting for the actions of popular fictional characters such as C.S.Forrester's naval hero Horatio Hornblower and Bernard Cornwell's rifleman Richard Sharpe. However, perhaps less well known is that the wars which followed in the wake of the French Revolution of 1789 were the focus of some of the world's greatest cartoonists, making this period part of 'The Golden Age of Caricature'.

Beginning in 1792, the French Revolutionary Wars became known as the Napoleonic Wars after Napoleon Bonaparte became First Consul of France seven years later. Following the execution of King Louis XVI in 1793 and France's invasion of the Netherlands, Britain (and, soon afterwards, Spain) joined the Allies and over the next two decades most countries in mainland Europe – as well as their dependent territories overseas – were involved in the conflicts. Indeed, seven separate international coalitions were formed to fight the French until the wars finally ended with the defeat of Napoleon in 1815.

It should be remembered that the Napoleonic Wars took place not only long before the invention of the Internet, DVDs, webcasts and emails but also before the personal computer, fax machine, television, radio, photography, cinema, the telephone and the international telegraph – not to mention motorcycles, automobiles and aeroplanes. This meant that news was very slow to reach the public and it was not until the Crimean War (1854-6) that the first war correspondents, war photographers and frontline war artists of any kind began to appear in any numbers. Added to which, daily and weekly newspapers were only printed in black-and-white and, until *The Times* published a woodcut of Nelson's funeral car in 1806, none carried any illustrations at all, let alone cartoons.

In the eighteenth and early nineteenth centuries, images of public figures and their activities were only available as expensive individual paintings or drawings or as relatively cheap mass-produced prints published by specialist companies. These prints, often hand-coloured, could be bought or hired, either from the publisher or from roadside caricature vendors. They could also be viewed for free in the printseller's own gallery, making printshop windows important sources of pictorial news and satire, especially in wartime. As one French émigré living in London reported in 1802: 'If men be fighting over there for their possessions and their bodies against the Corsican robber [Napoleon], they are fighting here to be first in Ackermann's shop and see Gillray's latest caricatures. The enthusiasm is indescribable when the next drawing appears; it is a veritable madness. You have to make your way in through the crowd with your fists...'

Technically, satirical drawings from this period ought not be described as cartoons. The word 'cartoon' (from the Italian *cartone*, meaning a sheet of paper or card, from which we also get the word 'carton') was originally applied to designs or templates for tapestries, mosaics or fresco paintings. Its more widely used modern sense dates from 1843 and derives from a *Punch* spoof by John Leech of a government-sponsored competition held that year for pictures to decorate the walls of the new Houses of Parliament. Classical-style cartoon designs sent in for the competition were exhibited in Westminster Hall and Leech attacked this as a waste of public money at a time when Londoners were starving. In a poignant satire he drew ragged and disabled figures attending the Westminster exhibition and headed his drawing 'Cartoon No.1: Substance and Shadow'. Five more drawings on social problems appeared over the following weeks (Cartoon Nos. 2-6) and thereafter the main weekly full-page topical drawing of the magazine was referred to as 'The Cartoon' (and its artist as

'The Cartoonist'). By association the word gradually came to be applied to comic or satirical drawings generally.

The art form itself, of course – generally known in the Napoleonic era as caricature (from another Italian word, *caricare*, meaning to overburden or exaggerate) – has a long history going back to Ancient Egypt. However, it became increasingly popular from the eighteenth century onwards. William Hogarth (1697-1764) is usually credited as being its founder in Britain and he was followed by two important amateurs, George (4th Viscount) Townshend (1724-1807) and Henry Bunbury (1750-1811), both of whom had their sketches reworked by professional artists and produced as prints.

Though a few limited-circulation (and short-lived) satirical magazines were published during the Napoleonic Wars – such as *The Satirist* (1807-12), *The Scourge* (1811-16) and *The Meteor* (1813-14) in Britain, and *Le Nain Jaune* (The Yellow Dwarf, 1814-1815) in France – it was the rapid expansion of the market for prints that gave graphic artists during this period their main outlet. Amongst the many publishers in London at this time there were five particularly celebrated printsellers: Hannah Humphrey in St James's Street (a short distance from St James's Palace, court of George III); Samuel Fores (who jokingly called himself 'Caricaturist to the First Consul' [i.e. Napoleon]) in Piccadilly; Rudolph Ackermann in the Strand near the law courts; Thomas Tegg in the then fashionable shopping and market district of Cheapside; and William Holland in Cockspur Street (near what would later be christened Trafalgar Square). In France one of the best known printshops was Martinet in Rue du Coq, Paris, and in Germany a celebrated caricature publisher was Frederick Campe of Nuremberg.

With all these new outlets came new artists. In Britain these included James Gillray, Thomas Rowlandson, Isaac Cruikshank, George Cruikshank, Charles Ansell (Charles Williams), George Woodward, William Elmes and William Heath. Amongst the notable foreign cartoonists of the period were the Germans Johann Michael Voltz and Johann Gottfried Schadow, and the Russian Ivan Terebenev. However, it was not until Napoleon's fateful Russian campaign of 1812 that a long ban on caricature in Russia was lifted, and there were very few German drawings on the wars before the French were defeated at Leipzig in 1813. As for France itself, most artists tended to remain anonymous. One of the main reasons for this was that from Bonaparte's appointment as First Consul until the end of the Empire strict censorship was imposed on the media, and comic sketches of Napoleon were punishable as *lèse-majesté*. This also applied to the many countries, such as Spain, Portugal and Italy (as well as their possessions overseas) which were ruled by the French empire, though David Hess (Switzerland), W.Esser (Holland) and others in occupied Europe did produce some powerful drawings.

Napoleon himself, like Robespierre before him, was very aware of the power of caricature and in 1805 wrote to Joseph Fouché, his Minister of Police: 'Have caricatures made: An Englishman, purse in hand, entreating the various Powers to take his money, &c...The immense attention which the English direct to gaining time by false news shows the extreme importance of this work.' Napoleon was also apparently much amused by Gillray's cartoon about the Peace of Amiens 'The First Kiss This Ten Years' (1803) but was upset and angered by his more personal attacks, notably 'The Handwriting on the Wall' (1803) and 'The Grand Coronation Procession of Napoleon the 1st, Emperor of France' (1805).

Napoleon Bonaparte was the most lampooned figure of his time. The first French caricature to feature him ('Little Coblenz', by Jean-Baptiste Isabey) was published in 1795 – before he came to power – and the first engraved portraits of him began to arrive in London in 1796. The first British caricature of Napoleon was credited to Isaac Cruikshank in 1797 and over the next two decades nearly 1000 prints featuring him were produced in Britain alone.

The diminutive emperor was a gift to cartoonists and after James Gillray transformed him into the Lilliputian character 'Little Boney' in 1803 – a belligerent, ranting midget wearing a huge tricorn hat – he became a stock figure of fun. He also also appeared in a wide variety of grotesque incarnations – from ape, serpent and dragon to earwig, toadstool and crocodile – forever battling John Bull, Britannia and the British Bulldog as well as the Russian bear and the Austrian and Prussian eagles.

Gillray's 'The Plumb-pudding in Danger' (1805) – featuring British Prime Minister William Pitt and Little Boney carving up the globe in the form of a Christmas pudding – is not only one of the best known political cartoons of all time but is also one of the most parodied. Indeed, it is still being adapted today as a vehicle for cartoonists worldwide to attack the ambitions of political leaders of all kinds.

The Allied monarchs and military commanders were also custom-made for caricature. The Duke of Wellington's nose, the Prussian Field Marshal Blücher's flamboyant moustache, the one-armed Lord Nelson with his eye-patch, the pug-faced (and mad) Tsar Paul of Russia, the club-footed French statesman Talleyrand, the portly Prince of Wales (later the Prince Regent), the abstemious George III ('Farmer George'), the wiry Prime Minister William 'Bottomless' Pitt (complete with pink spot to show his liking for port) and the wily, dark-jowled Opposition leader, Charles James Fox (often drawn as a fox), all featured prominently in prints produced both in Britain and overseas.

Such was the popularity of these satirical drawings that many of the leading figures of the day – including Wellington and Nelson – even bought caricatures themselves. On one occasion in the autumn of 1805 Nelson entered Samuel Fores' shop and, seeing the printseller's pregnant wife, is reputed to have declared: 'If it's a boy, Mrs Fores, damme, I'll be his godfather.' Nelson was killed soon afterwards at the Battle of Trafalgar but the child was christened Horatio Nelson Fores (in 1814 another son was called Arthur Blücher Fores in honour of Wellington – whose first name was Arthur – and the famous Prussian field marshal).

As there was no conscription in Britain during this period, very few professional cartoonists saw frontline action. However, George Cruikshank was a member of the Loyal North Britons, a volunteer regiment made up of Scots in London, and took part in the Grand Review in Hyde Park in 1814 at which the Prince Regent and Tsar Alexander I of Russia were present. As for James Gillray, not only was he the son of a soldier who had lost an arm in the war of the Austrian Succession, but he was also present in Flanders during the Duke of York's campaign in 1793, drawing on-the-spot portraits of the Allied commanders for Philippe de Loutherbourg's painting 'The Grand Attack on Valenciennes'. He was thus the first ever official war cartoonist.

Artists on both sides also produced illustrations for books, and many anti-French cartoons appeared on ceramics (especially domestic pottery such as jugs, mugs and tobacco jars). However, I have concentrated mainly on prints in this graphic scrapbook of the Napoleonic Wars for the simple reason that these would have been the most widely available to the general public. Sadly, like newspapers and magazines, a great many of these have vanished or been destroyed over the past two hundred years. Hence the present compendium which, it is hoped, will preserve some of them for posterity.

THE EARLY YEARS

AFTER THE OUTBREAK of the French Revolution in 1789, there was great anxiety in Europe about the spread of republicanism, especially following initial successes by the French Revolutionary Army against Prussia and Austria, the invasion of the Netherlands and the execution of King Louis XVI. France declared war on Britain on 1 February 1793 and on Spain soon afterwards, leading both countries to join Prussia and Austria in the First Coalition. One of the first major actions was the siege of the important Mediterranean naval base of Toulon which had remained loyal to the French monarchy and had been occupied by the British. In September, an artillery attack by a junior Corsican officer serving in the French Army, Napoleone Buonaparte, drove the British out and earnt him the rank of Brigadier-General. Meanwhile, Britain's Commander-in-Chief, the Duke of York, led an expeditionary force to help defend the Netherlands, joining up with the other Allies and capturing Valenciennes on the French border before being forced to retreat in 1794. However, the same year, during the war's first major naval engagement, the Royal Navy under Admiral Howe beat the French in the Atlantic in a battle known as 'The Glorious First of June'. Then in 1795 in the famous incident described by Carlyle as the 'whiff of grapeshot', Buonaparte was asked by the leaders of the new French government to disperse a pro-monarchist mob in Paris. As a result, he was appointed commander of the Army of Italy where (changing the spelling of his name to the more familiar, French-sounding, Napoleon Bonaparte) he won a series of victories against the Austrians. After some abortive attempts to land in Ireland and Wales the French government then put him in command of the Army of England with the intention of invading Britain. However, he decided instead to attack Egypt, part of the Turkish Ottoman Empire, with a view to denying the British access to the overland route to their colonies in India. At first he succeeded, defeating the Mameluke rulers of Egypt at the Battle of the Pyramids and elsewhere, but lost his fleet to a daring action by the British Admiral Nelson in Aboukir Bay near Alexandria in what became known as the Battle of the Nile. In an attempt to defeat the Turks Bonaparte then marched into the Holy Land, took Jaffa and laid siege to Acre but eventually abandoned his troops to return to Paris where he staged a *coup d'état*, dissolved the government and became one of three consuls ruling France.

French Liberty, British Slavery
James Gillray, 21 December 1792

The execution of Louis XVI in the Place de la Révolution (formerly the Place Louis XV and today the Place de la Concorde), Paris, on 21 January 1793 was deeply felt worldwide. Many viewed the French revolutionaries as a blood-thirsty rabble and there were great fears that the movement might spread to other countries.

In the first drawing (*opposite*) by James Gillray (1756-1815) – which was also copied in Germany and France – the artist contrasts the starving Frenchman eating garlic with the fat Englishman carving roast beef , a theme in British cartoons that harks back to William Hogarth (1697-1764) and 'The Gate of Calais – O The Roast Beef of Old England'. Gillray's second drawing (*right*), entitled 'A View in Perspective', marks the execution of King Louis XVI. The king – known as 'Citizen Capet' to the revolutionaries – can be seen on the guillotine while a church burns behind. A bishop and two monks hang from the building in the foreground while a Jacobin *sans-culotte* plays the fiddle and the crowd, all wearing the Liberty cap (or *bonnet rouge*), cheer on the executioner. The subtitle of the drawing is 'Religion, Justice, Loyalty and all the Bugbears of Unenlighten'd Minds, Farewell!' This cartoon was published less than a fortnight after France declared war on Britain on 1 February 1793. The other two drawings by Isaac Cruikshank (1764-1811) (*below right*) and Thomas Rowlandson (1756-1827) lampoon the citizens of the new French Republic. In the drawing by Cruikshank the ribbon in the woman's hair reads 'War, Eternal War' and in the background can be seen an inn with the head of Louis XVI as its sign.

The Zenith of French Glory – the Pinnacle of Liberty
James Gillray, 12 February 1793

A Democrat
Thomas Rowlandson, 2 September 1791

A Republican Belle – A Picture of Paris for 1794
Isaac Cruikshank, 10 March 1794

Fatigues of the Campaign in Flanders
James Gillray, 20 May 1793

The French occupied Brussels in November 1792 and invaded Holland in February 1793. The first military action by the British was to send an expeditionary force of 2000 men (four battalions of Guards) to the Netherlands to join the Allied army there. Its Commander-in-Chief was George III's second son, the 29-year-old Frederick Augustus, Duke of York (who had married the daughter of King Frederick William II of Prussia in 1791). Under the supreme command of the Austrians, the Allies then drove back the French in Flanders and the Duke of York's troops succeeded in capturing the fortified town of Valenciennes on the French side of the border with Belgium on 28 July 1793. However, after the battle of Tourcoing in May 1794 the Austrians fell back to the Rhine and the British were forced to retreat from the Netherlands. (This led to the popular children's rhyme, 'The Grand Old Duke of York, he had ten thousand men, he marched them up to the top of a hill and he marched them down again...') The remains of the original British invasion force sailed back from Bremen in April 1795.

The Military Caricaturist
James Gillray, 6 December 1799

The Archduke
James Gillray, 15 November 1796

The British Neptune Riding Triumphant, or the Carmagnols Dancing to the Tune of 'Rule Britannia'
Isaac Cruikshank, 16 June 1794

James Gillray – himself the son of a soldier who had lost an arm in Flanders during the war of the Austrian Succession – was present in Flanders during this campaign as he had been invited by the painter Philippe de Loutherbourg RA (1740-1812) to draw portraits of the Allied commanders for his painting *The Grand Attack on Valenciennes*. Thus Gillray became the first ever official war cartoonist and his 'Fatigues' drawing (*opposite top*), lampooning the lavish lifestyle of the Allied commanders, has some truth in it. As well as the Duke of York himself Austrian and Dutch officers (including the Prince of Orange) can be seen disporting themselves with Flemish women while starving soldiers serve them. 'The Archduke' (*opposite bottom right*) is a portrait of Archduke Charles (Karl Ludwig) – brother of Emperor Francis II of Austria and Governor of the Austrian Netherlands (modern Belgium) – who took part in the defence of the Netherlands and later emerged as Austria's greatest general.

While the British Army retreated through the Netherlands in the summer of 1794, there was cause for celebration at sea. On 'The Glorious First of June' 1794, the Royal Navy's Channel Fleet under Admiral Richard 'Black Dick' Howe beat the French in the Atlantic in the war's first major naval engagement, capturing seven warships escorting a merchant convoy and sinking another.

The drawing by Isaac Cruikshank (*above*) has Earl Howe as Neptune in a chariot drawn by dolphins which can be seen towing away French ships captured by the British as others retreat to the French naval base at Brest. A *carmagnole* was both a song (and dance) popular during the French Revolution and the name of the outfit that Frenchmen wore – a short jacket, black trousers, red Liberty cap and tricolour sash.

13

Taking Physick, or the News of Shooting the King of Sweden!
James Gillray, 11 April 1792

George III had been king of Great Britain and Ireland since 1760. He also ruled over Britain's many colonies worldwide and in addition was Elector of Hanover, one of the many independent German states that formed part of the electorate of the Holy Roman Empire administered by Austria. At a time of great revolutionary tensions – King Gustav III of Sweden was assassinated in March 1792 and George himself had survived a stabbing attempt in 1786 – he watched developments in France with great anxiety but with considerable courage, vowing that he would lead the country in battle if the French invaded Britain.

In Gillray's first cartoon (*above*) British Prime Minister William Pitt brings the news of the death of King Gustav ('Another Monarch done over!') to George III and Queen Charlotte as they sit on the lavatory. The second (*right*), has the king examining a miniature portrait (by Samuel Cooper) of Oliver Cromwell, ruler of Britain after the execution of King Charles I following the English Revolution of the previous century. In the well-known print (*opposite top*), commenting on the frugal habits of the royal couple, the king is wearing a sword and his 'Windsor Uniform' (which he had introduced 12 years earlier). A less pleasant image is the caricature print (*opposite bottom*) by the famous French painter Jacques-Louis David (1774-1825), in which George's head appears as the bottom of a devilish monster labelled 'the English government' which blasts the 'free-born' English.

A Connoisseur Examining a Cooper
James Gillray, 18 June 1792

Temperance Enjoying a Frugal Meal
James Gillray, 28 July 1792

The English Government
Jacques-Louis David, c.1794

Napoleon Working the Gun at Toulon
George Cruikshank in 'Dr Syntax' (William Combe), *The Life of Napoleon* (1815)

Despite the Revolution there were still Royalist strongholds in France, especially in the south of the country. One of these was the major Mediterranean naval base of Toulon which had remained loyal to the French monarchy and had been occupied by the British under Lord Hood. As a result it was besieged by the Republicans and in September 1794 an artillery attack by a 24-year-old Corsican officer serving in the French Army, Napoleone Buonaparte, drove out the British who set fire to the French fleet as they left. This was the first time Buonaparte had come to public notice (the action earned him promotion to the rank of Brigadier-General) and though no cartoons were published about the incident at the time, many drawings were later produced to commemorate the event.

The first shown here (*top*) is by Isaac Cruikshank's oldest son George (1792-1878) from a life of Napoleon in verse by William Combe who had earlier written the text for the famous 'Dr Syntax' books illustrated by Thomas Rowlandson. In this drawing Buonaparte is shown firing a mortar while in the much later French version (*below*) by Job (Jacques Onfroy de Bréville, 1858-1931) he loads a cannon.

The Battery of the Men Without Fear
Job in Jules de Marthold's *Le Grand Napoleon des Petits Enfants* (1893)

Buonaparte at Rome Giving Audience in State
Isaac Cruikshank, 17 March 1797

The French Bugabo Frightening the Royal Commanders
Isaac Cruikshank, 14 April 1797

Since the Revolution the French Republic had been ruled by the National Convention consisting of 750 deputies, who were later dominated by the lawyer Maximilien Robespierre and his Committee of Public Safety. However, after the fall of Robespierre there were a number of demonstrations against the new government and its executive of five directors (the Directory) elected by the two legislative chambers – the Council of Elders and the Council of Five Hundred. When a Royalist mob in Paris rose in a major revolt the Directory ordered Buonaparte to disperse the crowd with artillery – killing or injuring more than 500. This incident, which took place on 26 October 1795 (13 Vendémiaire, Year III, in the Revolutionary calendar), was famously described by the historian Thomas Carlyle in his book *The French Revolution: A History* (1837) as the 'whiff of grapeshot' (after the type of ammunition used, which consisted of small iron balls). In March 1796 the Directory appointed Buonaparte commander of the Army of Italy. Here he won a series of spectacular victories against the Allied army in northern Italy – notably at Lodi, Arcola, Bassano, Rivoli and Castiglione – and by the Treaty of

Tolentino in February 1797 Pope Pius VI agreed to the establishment of a French-ruled puppet state, the Cisalpine Republic. At about this time Buonaparte also changed his name from the Italianate Napoleone Buonaparte to the more familiar, and French-sounding, Napoleon Bonaparte.

'Buonaparte at Rome' (*top*) was the first British cartoon to feature Bonaparte and shows him in the Vatican, being offered the keys of Rome by Pope Pius VI. (In fact this is historically incorrect as Bonaparte, though rumoured to be in Rome, was actually at Ancona.) The second of Cruikshank's drawings has Bonaparte riding a 'bugaboo' (a bugbear or dragon) whose fiery breath contains guns and soldiers (note the Pope beneath it at the left), frightening off Archduke Charles of Austria and the Duke of York (neither of whom actually took part in the Italian campaign), and their armies. Above them the winged head of the pro-French British politician Charles James Fox smiles down on the Allied generals (most of whom had been defeated by Bonaparte) and tells them to run.

17

The Political Locust
Isaac Cruikshank, 14 August 1795

Britain's Prime Minister at the outbreak of the French Revolutionary Wars was William Pitt the Younger. The second son of the great British Prime Minister William Pitt the Elder, Earl of Chatham, he became Chancellor of the Exchequer in 1782 and Prime Minister in 1783 (aged 24), governing Britain for the next 17 years. However, he was not universally liked, especially after the introduction of income tax in 1799 to pay for the war against France.

Cruikshank has Pitt as a locust (*above*) eating the remains of 'Poor Old England' as Britain is hit by food shortages and new taxes. The anonymous French drawing (*right*) and the colour print (*opposite top right*) by the Irish artist William O'Keefe (fl.1800s) both allude to the close relationship between Pitt and George III (a keen farmer, the king was affectionately known as 'Farmer George'). Gillray's first drawing (*opposite top left*) goes a step further and has Pitt as a toadstool growing out of the Crown in a criticism of his use of the corrupt system of royal patronage. 'Presages of the Millennium' (*opposite bottom*) depicts Pitt as the classical figure of Death on a pale horse riding over Edmund Burke's 'swinish multitude' (the general public) and kicking away Fox, Sheridan, Wilberforce and other Opposition advocates of peace with France.

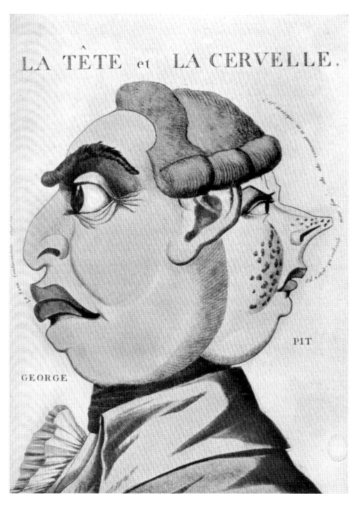

The Head and the Brain
French print, 1804

An Excrescence – a Fungus, alias a Toadstool Upon a Dunghill
James Gillray, 20 December 1791

Farmer George's Wonderful Monkey
William O'Keefe, 2 July 1795

Presages of the Millennium, with the Destruction of the Faithful
James Gillray, 4 June 1795

19

In the face of increasing threats from France, Parliament had called for the raising of volunteer militias nationwide in April 1794. One of the first to be formed was based on the parish of St George's Church, Hanover Square (south of Oxford Circus), in London.

**Supplementary Militia, Turning Out for Twenty Days' Amusement –
'The French Invade Us, Hey? Damme Who's Afraid?'**
James Gillray, 25 November 1796

**St George's Volunteers Charging Down Bond Street After Clearing
the Ring in Hyde Park and Storming the Dunghill at Marylebone**
James Gillray, 1 March 1797

Heroes Recruiting at Kelsey's, or Guard Day at St James's
James Gillray, 9 June 1797

General Complaint
British print, 1796

As well as volunteer regiments, many new recruits joined the regular army, with commissions being bought by rich families for their sons. In 'Heroes Recruiting at Kelsey's' (*above left*) the allusion is to Kelsey's famous sweetshop in St James's, London. Gillray has drawn three very unlikely soldiers – one fat, one very tall and one extremely young (left, eating sugar plums) in criticism of the system of purchase of commissions. 'General Complaint' (*above right*) has much the same message.

A Puzzle of Portraits, or the Hour Glass Exhausted
Isaac Cruikshank, 10 February 1794

**The French Invasion, or John Bull
Bombarding the Bum-Boats**
British print, 5 November 1793

After the defeat of the Allies in Flanders there was a very real fear that the French would invade Britain as forecast earlier in *Reflections on the Revolution in France* (1790) by the distinguished statesman and political philosopher Edmund Burke. There was also concern lest the many French émigrés arriving in Britain might include revolutionary 'banditti' in disguise.

'A Puzzle of Portraits' (*above left*) shows an hourglass made of the profiles of Pitt (left) and George III, set in a frame of human bones, with the implication that time is running out for

Britain. In 'The French Invasion' (*above right*) the map of England and Wales has been transformed into the body of George III who defecates, from the Royal Navy base at Portsmouth, on the French invasion fleet. Gillray (*opposite top*) imagines French troops marching through the streets of London as Pitt is flogged after being tied to a pole topped by the French cap of Liberty. Richard Newton (1777-98), meanwhile (*opposite bottom*), has Pitt riding on the back of George III depicted as an enormous bugbear shouting defiance.

**Promised Horrors of the French Invasion, or Forcible Reasons
for Negotiating a Regicide Peace – *vide the Authority of Edmund Burke***
James Gillray, 20 October 1796

A Bugaboo
Richard Newton, 1792

23

French Ambassador, Executed by Citizen Fox
British print, 18 December 1792

**Fashion Before Ease, or A Good Constitution Sacrificed
for a Fantastick Form**
James Gillray, 2 January 1793

It should not be forgotten that at first there were many sympathisers with the French Revolution in Britain. Amongst them were supporters of Thomas Paine, the radical pamphleteer who after the publication of Burke's *Reflections* wrote a famous rejoinder, *The Rights of Man* (1791-2), and later fled to France where he became a Deputy for Pas de Calais. One of the most ardent opponents of the war with France was the eminent politician Charles James Fox (some even saw Fox's support for the French cause as close to treason and accused him of being a French spy).

'Fashion Before Ease' (*above left*) alludes to the fact that Paine was a former staymaker (a manufacturer of corsets) and he is shown wearing a French *bonnet rouge* and trying to fit Britannia (holding on to a British oak tree) into a 'fashionable' French corset.

The anonymous print 'French Ambassador' (*above right*) is highly critical of Fox and even calls him 'Citizen Fox' after the French manner. In 'French Telegraph' (*opposite top*), Fox has been transformed into a giant version of the newly invented semaphore telegraph, shining a light to attract the French fleet with one hand while pointing at St Paul's Cathedral and London with the other. Meanwhile, Cruikshank (*opposite bottom*) illustrates one of the more popular of the many wild rumours that circulated about how the French forces would invade Britain, ranging from tunnels under the Channel to giant hot-air balloons. It shows a huge French troop-carrying raft powered by windmill-driven paddles being winched across the Channel by Fox and his friends as Pitt and two colleagues blow up a storm.

French Telegraph Making Signals in the Dark
James Gillray, 26 January 1795

The Raft in Danger, or the Republican Crew Disappointed
Isaac Cruikshank, 28 January 1798

Prepared for a French Invasion
William O'Keefe, 1 October 1796

End of the Irish Invasion, or The Destruction of the French Armada
James Gillray, 20 January 1797

After the French had assembled an invasion force under General Lazare Hoche – then Bonaparte's main rival as French military leader – their first plan was to attack southern Ireland. In so doing they hoped to foment an uprising by Wolfe Tone's 'United Irishmen' and others who wished the country to become a separate republic (the United Kingdom of Great Britain and Ireland was not established until 1800). The invasion force consisted of 15,000 French troops in numerous transports. It sailed from Brest on 15 December 1796 escorted by 20 frigates and 17 ships of the line but encountered stormy weather near its proposed landing spot at Bantry Bay, off the coast of County Cork in southwest Ireland, and had to disperse.

In the cartoon by the Irishman William O'Keefe (*top*), Pitt and King George – aided by a gang of old women – prepare to hold off a boatload of French devils brandishing a guillotine. The cartoon by Gillray (*above*) shows the storm at sea which dispersed the French invasion fleet much as it had done the Spanish Armada two centuries earlier. The faces blowing the four winds are those of (left to right): Pitt, Dundas (Secretary of State for War), Grenville (Foreign Secretary) and Windham (Secretary at War) and amongst the foundering ships is *Le Révolutionnaire* (centre) with Fox as its figurehead. Those in the Revolutionary Jolly Boat include the pro-Republican playwright and MP R.B.Sheridan (left) and Lord Erskine (third from left).

The Tables Turned
James Gillray, 4 March 1797

In February 1797, soon after the failure of the Irish invasion, 1400 French irregulars known as the *Légion Noire* (Black Legion), under the American Colonel Tate, attempted to land on the Pembrokeshire coast of Wales but were captured by the local militia. News also reached Britain at about this time of the success (on 14 February) of Sir John Jervis in defeating the Spanish fleet off Cape St Vincent in southern Portugal, thereby preventing them from joining the French and Dutch fleets in a planned combined attack on Britain. There were also celebrations in Britain later in the year at the news of the premature death (of natural causes) aged 31 of General Hoche on 19 September and the destruction of the Dutch fleet by Admiral Duncan at the Battle of Camperdown on 11 October.

Gillray's drawing (*above*) has the tables turned on the devil Fox as he celebrates the French landing in Wales but then learns from 'Billy Pitt' the news of the British success at the Battle of Cape St Vincent. 'The Apotheosis of Hoche' (*right*) – with the French general in the centre holding a guillotine like a lyre – is probably one of the most elaborate cartoons ever drawn.

The Apotheosis of Hoche
James Gillray, 11 January 1798

The Military Committee
David Hess/James Gillray, 1796

Some of the Representatives of the People of Holland
David Hess/James Gillray, 1796

Consequences of a Successful French Invasion – Plate No.1.
'We come to recover your long lost Liberties.' *Scene: The House of Commons*
James Gillray, 1 March 1798

'Push Hard, Swiss Gold Will Buy Us Egypt'
Swiss print, c.1798

After the retreat of the Allies from the Netherlands in 1795 the Dutch royal family fled to Britain. The French Revolutionary Army quickly occupied Holland and set up a Republican puppet state named the Batavian Republic with a French naval base at Flushing (Vlissingen) on the south coast of Walcheren Island, commanding the estuary of the River Scheldt and access to the major port of Antwerp.

The first two of the drawings opposite (*top left and right*) are part of a series of 20 propaganda prints etched by Gillray and later published in book form in London as *Hollandia Regenerata*. Based on the original drawings of the Swiss caricaturist David Hess (1770-1843) – who had served as a soldier in the Dutch Army – they showed the hardships of life in the Netherlands under the French occupation and were produced with captions in Dutch, French and English for distribution overseas. Such was the impact of these prints that Sir John Dalrymple commissioned a similar series of 20

from Gillray entitled 'Consequences of a Successful French Invasion'. However, only four of these appeared, one of which is shown here (*opposite bottom*) – note Pitt and others in chains.

In 1798 Switzerland was also occupied by France and renamed the Helvetic Republic. It too suffered financial privations as a result, especially to fund new French military campaigns. After the death of Hoche, the French government put Bonaparte in charge of the Army of England but he later convinced them to abandon the project in the short term to concentrate on an attack on Egypt (then ruled by the Turkish Ottoman Empire) with a view to cutting off Britain's route to India.

In the Swiss drawing (*above*) the members of the French Directory are seen squeezing a rock labelled 'Berne' in a press to extract gold to pay for the Egyptian expedition (note the map of Egypt on the wall). Similar boulders marked 'Zurich' and 'Vaud' await their turn.

Bonaparte sailed from Toulon on 19 May 1798 with 13 ships of the line, 7 frigates, 62 gunboats and 400 transport vessels containing 20,000 troops – the 'Army of the Orient' – and other personnel. He occupied neutral Malta on 12 June and – without declaring war on Turkey – successfully landed his invasion force in Alexandria on 1 July, anchoring his fleet in the apparent safety of the deep-water harbour at Aboukir Bay at the mouth of the River Nile. Leaving garrisons in Alexandria and nearby Rosetta he then marched southeast towards Cairo. On 21 July he reached Embaba on the left bank of the Nile, opposite Cairo, where he was met by the Mameluke forces of the Sultan of Turkey. Preparing for battle, Bonaparte is alleged to have said to his troops, as he pointed to the Pyramids: 'Soldiers, forty centuries look down upon you!' The Battle of the Pyramids (21 July 1798) resulted in a victory for the French who occupied Cairo soon afterwards.

The drawing (*right*) is typical of the popular prints known as *Les images d'Epinal* produced in the town of Epinal in eastern France.

The Battle of the Pyramids
French Epinal print, c.1798

Extirpation of the Plagues of Egypt – Destruction of Revolutionary Crocodiles, or the British Hero Cleansing ye Mouth of ye Nile
James Gillray, 6 October 1798

John Bull Taking a Luncheon, or British Cooks Cramming Old Grumble-Gizzard with *Bonne-Chère*
James Gillray, 24 October 1798

A week after the Battle of the Pyramids, while Bonaparte was consolidating his hold over Egypt, ships of the Royal Navy under Admiral Nelson, in an audacious attack, destroyed the French fleet moored near Alexandria at the Battle of the Nile (also called the Battle of Aboukir Bay) on 1 August 1798, leaving Bonaparte cut off from France. During the battle the huge French flagship, *L'Orient*, caught fire and exploded.

In Gillray's first cartoon (*left*), the by now one-eyed and one-armed Nelson – wielding a club of 'British oak' (from which his ships were made) – blows up one French crocodile (representing *L'Orient*), beats others senseless, and tows a number of others away on hooks and lines. In the background can be seen the Pyramids. In Gillray's second drawing (*bottom*) Nelson (foreground, right) and his fellow admirals – Warren, Earl Howe, Viscount Bridport (formerly Hood), Duncan, Gardiner and Earl St Vincent (formerly Jervis) – serve up French 'frigasees' (frigates/ *fricassées*) while British anti-war politicians Fox and Sheridan can be seen cursing his success through the window.

Fighting for the Dunghill, or Jack Tar Settling Buonaparte
James Gillray, 20 November 1798

The defeat at the Battle of the Nile was a major blow for the French. In Gillray's 'The Fight for the Dunghill' (*above*) note that where the British Jack Tar (the Royal Navy's equivalent of John Bull) has hit Bonaparte in the belly he has left the imprint of the name 'Nelson'. In the gruesome drawing, 'Destruction of the French Colossus' (*right*), the reference is to the huge 100-foot-tall bronze statue to the sun-god Helios that stood in the harbour in Rhodes in ancient times, one of the Seven Wonders of the World. Note that it is Britannia's thunderbolt that destroys the Colossus which has Louis XVI's head around its neck and tramples on a bible, a crucifix and a pair of scales (of justice).

Destruction of the French Colossus
James Gillray, 1 November 1798

The State of the War, or the Monkey Race in Danger
James Gillray, 20 May 1799

Allied Powers *Unbooting* Egalité
James Gillray, 1 September 1799

General Swallow Destroying the French Army – *talk of Gulliver's carrying off fifty ships at once, why it was nothing to him!*
Isaac Cruikshank, 1 June 1799

The Second Coalition against France was formed in June 1799. Its members were Britain, Austria, Naples, Russia and Turkey. Apart from the battles against Bonaparte's forces in Egypt and those of the Royal Navy at sea, there were also conflicts in the Netherlands (the Duke of York – by now Commander-in-Chief of the British Army – led an Anglo-Russian force to try and evict the French) and Germany (where the Austrians were led by Archduke Charles). However, though these resulted in defeat for the Allies, they had better fortune in northern Italy. Here a Russo-Austrian army led by the very tall (6 feet 10 inches) but elderly Russian Field Marshal Alexander Suvarov undid much of the success the French had achieved earlier, with spectacular victories at Cassano D'Adda (27 April), Turin (26 May), Trebbia (17-19 June) and elsewhere – which won Suvarov the title 'Prince of Italy'.

In Gillray's first cartoon (*opposite top*) he portrays the French troops as monkeys being put to flight by (left to right) a Turkish monster (note the crescent head), a Russian bear, an Austrian eagle and (in the foreground) a British lion. In 'Allied Powers' (*opposite bottom*), Russia and Austria are seen removing the boot of Italy from Bonaparte while a Turk is about to slice off his nose to add to the ears and noses already strung around his neck. Britain's Jack Tar holds Bonaparte's arms while a Dutchman tries to grab a Dutch Cheese from under his feet. Cruikshank, meanwhile (*above*), plays on Suvarov's name (which was then also spelt 'Suwarrow') and alludes to Jonathan Swift's satire *Gulliver's Travels* (1726), in which Gulliver in the land of the tiny Lilliputians seems to be a huge monster. (Suvarov was later defeated by the French at the Second Battle of Zurich on 25 September 1799 and died in St Petersburg in 1800.)

Field Marshal Count Suwarrow-Rominskoy
James Gillray, May 1799

'Siege de la Colonne de Pompée' – Science in the Pillory
James Gillray, 6 March 1799

When Bonaparte left Toulon for Egypt he took with him more than 150 'savants' – including engineers, botanists, archaeologists, mathematicians, naturalists and poets – and the Institute d'Egypte was founded in Cairo on 23 August 1798. One of the most famous discoveries of the French scientists was the Rosetta Stone (the key to deciphering Egyptian hieroglyphics).

The two drawings shown here allude to the publication in London of a series of intercepted letters from French officers complaining about the situation in Egypt. The first (*left*) has a group of savants trapped on top of the 114-feet-tall Pompey's Column in Alexandria as they are besieged by Turkish troops, while the second (*below*) has two naturalists being chased by crocodiles as they try to put saddles and bridles on them.

'L'Insurrection de L'Institut Amphibie' – the Pursuit of Knowledge
James Gillray, 12 March 1799

Sir Sidney Smith
James Gillray, 10 November 1799

Cut off in Egypt, Bonaparte prepared to face two Turkish armies being assembled to attack him – one in Syria and one on the island of Rhodes – and decided to march into the Holy Land, en route to the Turkish capital of Constantinople (Istanbul). After taking Gaza he attacked Jaffa, which fell on 6 March 1799, and received much international criticism for the massacre of 4000 prisoners-of-war four days later. Then on 21 March he laid siege to the fortress town of Acre (north of Haifa) which barred the coastal road and was seen as the key to Syria and the Holy Land. Here he was also confronted by a British naval squadron under Sir Sidney Smith which attacked Bonaparte's supply lines, captured French guns and kept the fortress provisioned. After 61 days, with nearly 5000 French killed, wounded or sick, Bonaparte finally abandoned the siege on 20 May. This was Bonaparte's first major defeat on land and the only one he would suffer until Aspern-Essling in May 1809 (see p.93).

The Siege of Acre
George Cruikshank in William Combe, *The Life of Napoleon* (1815)

George Cruikshank in William Combe, *The Life of Napoleon* (1815)

After his defeat at Acre, Bonaparte then retraced his tracks. In Jaffa his troops caught the plague (it was later alleged that Bonaparte had poisoned 500 of his own men with opium) but he eventually reached Egypt. Here, at the Battle of Aboukir (25 July 1799), he defeated a Turkish army of 15,000 troops led by Mustapha Pasha which had been sent from Rhodes. Soon afterwards he learnt that France was in crisis after defeats by Austria in Germany and by Russia in Italy. As a result, without awaiting official recall orders from the French government, he abandoned his army and secretly returned to France on 22 August 1799, leaving General Jean-Baptiste Kléber in charge.

In both Cruikshank's and Gillray's drawings (*above and right*) of Bonaparte deserting his army note that he takes with him chests of Egyptian treasure, while Gillray (prophetically) also has him pointing to an imperial crown and sceptre.

The Deserter of the Army of Egypt
James Gillray, 8 March 1800

The Corsican Crocodile Dissolving the Council of Frogs!!!
British print, November 1799

**Exit Liberté à la François!, or Buonaparte Closing
the Farce of Egalité at St Cloud near Paris, Nov 10 1799**
James Gillray, 21 November 1799

Bonaparte landed at Fréjus in the south of France on 9 October 1799 and went straight to Paris. Here he found the members of the corrupt and unpopular Directory plotting against each other. Appointed commandant of the forces in the capital, he then made a bold move. With the aid of his older brother Lucien (who had recently been elected President of the Council of Five Hundred), he staged a *coup d'état* on 18 Brumaire, Year 8 (9 November 1799), dissolved the Directory and dispersed the Council of Five Hundred with armed troops. (For most observers, including the international cartoonists, this was seen to be the end of the French Republic and the beginning of a dictatorship ruled by Bonaparte.)

The anonymous British cartoon (*top*) has Bonaparte as a huge crocodile (note that he is wearing a crown, already implying his imperial aspirations), supported by a group of armed crocodiles about to dissolve the Council of Five Hundred, portrayed as frogs. Gillray (*bottom*) shows a similar scene using human figures.

The Consular Trio
French print, 1799

The French Consular Triumvirate Settling the New Constitution – With a Peep at the Constitutional Pigeon-Holes of the Abbé Sieyès in the Background
James Gillray, 1 January 1800

After the *coup* of 18 Brumaire Bonaparte became one of three consuls in a provisional government ruling France. Bonaparte himself became First Consul (appointed for 10 years), the other two being Jean-Jacques Cambacérès (the former Minister of Justice) as Second Consul and the lawyer Charles-François Lebrun as Third Consul. On Christmas Day 1799, Bonaparte wrote a personal letter to George III suggesting peace terms. This was rejected in January 1800. The French Army then began a new campaign in Italy. After assembling 30,000 troops (the Army of the Reserve) in Switzerland, Bonaparte made his famous crossing of the Alps via the St Bernard Pass and arrived in Milan on 2 June. He then defeated the Austrians near Alessandria in northwestern Italy at the Battle of Marengo (14 June 1800) and later named his white horse and the chicken dish Poulet Marengo in its honour.

The French caricature (*above left*) – whose title translates literally as 'In the Sack' or 'In the Bag' – has the three new consuls (left to right), Cambacérès, Bonaparte and Lebrun combined into a single figure with three feet. Gillray's portrait of them (*above right*) 'settling the New Constitution' has Bonaparte sitting opposite Cambacérès and Lebrun while the Abbé Sieyès (a former Director who had supported the *coup*) is seen pulling apart the curtains at the back of the room to reveal pigeon-holes full of a variety of paper (i.e. bogus) constitutions.

The Outrage of the Rue Saint-Nicaise
French print, December 1800

Despite his military successes Bonaparte was not universally popular at home. On the evening of 24 December 1800 he narrowly escaped death in a Royalist assassination attempt when a bomb hidden in a water cart exploded as his carriage drove to the Opera along the Rue Saint-Nicaise in Paris en route to hear the first performance of Haydn's *The Creation*. Although the First Consul himself was unharmed, 20 people were killed and more than 50 were injured.

Tsar Paul of Russia was less fortunate. The son of Empress Catherine the Great and Tsar Peter III (who had himself been murdered), he had come to the throne on his mother's death in November 1796 but his often irrational behaviour led him to be known as 'the Mad Tsar'. On 23 March 1801, he was strangled in his bedroom at Mikhailovsky Castle, St Petersburg, and succeeded by his 25-year-old son Alexander I.

The French cartoon (*opposite bottom*) depicts the scene of the explosion in the Rue Saint-Nicaise. Meanwhile, Gillray's portrait of Tsar Paul of Russia (*right*), is actually a reissue of his earlier print from 1799 but with the addition of the island of Malta in the background. (Paul had originally declared war on France after Napoleon had occupied Malta – as he was Grand Master of the Knights of St John based there – but changed sides when Britain subsequently took the island.) The Latin phrase, a spoof of *Mens Sana in Corpore Sano* (a sound mind in a sound body) translates as 'Deformed in mind, deformed in body'. In Cruikshank's drawing (*below*) the image of Paul as a bear being led on a chain by Napoleon was originally accompanied by four verses of a ballad about the 'moonstruck Russian railer'.

The Magnanimous Ally – Painted at Petersburg
James Gillray, 20 January 1801

Crazy Paul!!
Isaac Cruikshank, 5 February 1801

1801-02

AFTER THE BATTLE of Marengo in Italy the Austrians also suffered a number of defeats by the French in Germany, notably at the Battle of Hohenlinden (3 December 1800). As a result Emperor Francis II sued for peace and on 9 February 1801 signed the Treaty of Lunéville. This left Britain to fight France alone (Russia had withdrawn from the Second Coalition in 1799). To break a crippling blockade not only by France but also by the newly formed 'Northern Alliance' – the League of Armed Neutrality of Russia, Sweden, Denmark and Prussia – Admiral Sir Hyde Parker led a successful raid on Copenhagen, the closest of the League's capitals. This, together with a change of attitude by the new Tsar of Russia, Alexander I, led to the end of the Northern Alliance.

Meanwhile, Ireland became part of the United Kingdom by the Act of Union (1801), and the Union Flag received its final addition, the red-on-white cross of St Patrick. However, the failure to allow Irish Catholic MPs to sit in Westminster led to the resignation of Pitt as Prime Minister (he was succeeded by Henry Addington). In Egypt, British troops landed and defeated the remains of the French Army of the Orient, cut off and deserted by Napoleon, at the Battle of Alexandria (21 March 1801) and the Royal Navy defeated the French at the two battles of Algeciras near Gibraltar in July. A stalemate then ensued and peace feelers began to be put out by both sides. The result was a ceasefire in October 1801 which would eventually lead to the signing of the Treaty of Amiens (1802).

In France – at peace for the first time in a decade – Bonaparte was elected First Consul for life (effectively making him sole dictator) and ceased to use his surname altogether, being known hereafter only as Napoleon. He also became the first President of a new Italian Republic formed from French conquests in the peninsula, which was enlarged later in 1802 by the annexation of the duchies of Piedmont, Parma and the island of Elba. In October 1802 Switzerland was also annexed by France.

Rarities from Abroad
British print, 18 March 1801

On 13 February 1801 the British government proclaimed a 'General Fast' to highlight shortages of food and other essentials denied by the blockade. Then, to break up the 'Northern Alliance', Britain made a pre-emptive strike on the Danish capital of Copenhagen without a declaration of war. The expedition was led by Admiral Sir Hyde Parker ('Old Vinegar') and the Battle of Copenhagen took place on 2 April 1801. Primarily a naval action between the two fleets, it also involved some British infantry. Admiral Horatio Nelson in HMS *Elephant* distinguished himself in the battle after ignoring an order from Parker to withdraw – famously putting his telescope to his blind eye and declaring that he had not see the

flag signal. Nearly all the 18 Danish ships in the harbour were burnt, captured or sunk. The action had the desired effect as the League was broken up soon afterwards.

'Rarities' (*above*) – published two weeks before the battle – is surprisingly prophetic. William Pitt (who the artist erroneously portrays as Prime Minister still, though Addington had taken over on 17 March) is seen leading a chained Tsar Paul of Russia as a muzzled bear with Napoleon on his head, followed by two more bears labelled 'Denmark' and 'Sweden' and (erroneously) a two-headed eagle labelled 'Prussia'. They are met by John Bull and his piper brother Andrew (representing Scotland).

The Battle of Copenhagen brought Nelson back into the public eye. A relative of former Prime Minister Sir Robert Walpole and the nephew of Captain Maurice Suckling (Comptroller of the Royal Navy), he had been married since 1787. However, there was considerable discussion of his on-going affair with the former artist's model Emma Hamilton, wife of the British Ambassador to the Kingdom of Naples, Sir William Hamilton. They had first met in Naples in 1793 but their relationship began when Nelson put into Naples harbour for repairs to his ships after the glorious victory of the Battle of the Nile in 1798. In January 1801, three months before the Battle of Copenhagen, Emma gave birth to their daughter, Horatia.

The cartoonists were quick to lampoon Nelson and Emma. Rowlandson (*top left*) shows her as an artist's model, while Gillray (*below*) depicts her as Dido, Queen of ancient Carthage, who (as related in Virgil's *Aeneid*) fell in love with the Greek Aeneas (hero of Troy and founder of Rome) after he was driven to Carthage by storms at sea, and died of grief at his departure. The portrait of Nelson (*top right*) emphasises his vanity by showing him wearing in his hat the diamond plume of triumph given him by the Sultan of Turkey after the Battle of the Nile (its centre revolved by clockwork power).

Lady Hxxxxxxx's Attitudes
Thomas Rowlandson, c.1800

The Hero of the Nile
James Gillray, 1 December 1798

Dido, in Despair!
James Gillray, 6 February 1801

William Pitt had resigned as Prime Minister in February 1801 and had been succeeded by his friend, the former Speaker of the House, Henry Addington. However, the new administration was not well received by the public and they appeared as minor figures compared to Pitt and his colleagues.

In Gillray's cartoon (*right*) Addington (left) is shown trying to fit into Pitt's huge hat, coat and boot, while Lord Hawkesbury (later himself Prime Minister, as Lord Liverpool) disappears into Grenville's huge trousers. Lord Hobart (centre with sword) cannot fill Dundas' kilt nor Lord Glenbervie (bottom right) Canning's slippers.

Lilliputian Substitutes, Equipping for Public Service
James Gillray, 28 May 1801

Preliminaries of Peace! or John Bull and His Little Friends 'Marching to Paris'
James Gillray, 6 October 1801

The Universal Toast
French print, 1802

Peace negotiations between Britain, France, Spain and Holland began in October 1801 and a treaty was finally signed in Amiens on the River Somme in northeastern France on 27 March 1802. Known to British satirists as the 'peace that passeth all understanding', the terms of the Treaty of Amiens dictated that Britain should restore to France, Spain and Holland all possessions occupied or conquered during the war, including Malta, the Cape of Good Hope and Egypt. The only exceptions were Trinidad and Ceylon (now Sri Lanka) which Britain was allowed to keep. For the first time in a decade there was peace, and British tourists flocked to Paris. However, as neither side honoured the commitments of the treaty it was seen in hindsight as merely a 13-month truce in what would be a war of 22 years. By May 1803 war had been declared again.

In Gillray's cartoon (*left*) Lord Hawkesbury (Foreign Secretary) is shown as a drummer boy holding an olive branch as he steps across a rotten-looking plank (labelled 'Heart of Oak') to France. Behind him is John Bull being led by tiny English Jacobins (notably Fox, left, blowing a trumpet). In the French cartoon (*below*), Napoleon (with his back to the viewer) lifts his glass for the toast while one of the representatives of the other nine Great Powers holds up a document marked 'General Peace'.

Two more views of the Peace of Amiens. In Gillray's first cartoon (*right*) – which apparently gave Napoleon much amusement but was somewhat out of date by the time of its publication – the thin Citizen François, with his hat and sword on the ground, kisses a plump and richly dressed Britannia, with her shield and trident behind her. They appear beneath portraits of Napoleon and George III. 'A Phantasmagoria' (*below*) has Addington (left), Fox (holding broom) and Hawkesbury as the witches from Shakespeare's *Macbeth* around a cauldron full of the remains of the British Lion (whose head can be seen in the foreground), beneath a crowing French cockerel. Kneeling in front of the pot is Pitt's friend the philanthropist William Wilberforce as a monk holding a 'Hymn of Peace', while behind is the skeleton of Britannia above whom floats a cloud inscribed 'PEACE'.

The First Kiss This Ten Years!, or the Meeting of Britannia & Citizen François
James Gillray, 1 January 1803

A Phantasmagoria
Scene: Conjuring up an Armed Skeleton
James Gillray, 5 January 1803

Introduction of Citizen Volpone & His Suite at Paris
James Gillray, 15 November 1802

Thousands of Britons visited France during the 13-month calm that followed the signing of the Treaty of Amiens. Amongst the politicians to be entertained by Napoleon at the Tuileries Palace in Paris was the pro-French Charles James Fox.

In the first cartoon by Gillray (*left*) Fox (*volpone* in Latin) is seen bowing to Napoleon on a throne whose arms end in globes. Either side of Napoleon stand Mameluke guards from Egypt. Fox claimed that the reason for his visit was to search the Paris archives for his history of James II (hence the 'original Jacobin manuscript' in his pocket). The other figures are (left to right) the exiled Irish patriot Arthur O'Connor, Mrs Armistead (Mrs Fox), Lord Erskine, Lady and Lord Holland (Fox's nephew) and (grovelling) the pro-French MP Robert Adair. In 'The Nursery' (*below*), a chubby Britannia sleeps in the cradle, rocked by Prime Minister Addington, while Fox washes nappies (of 'French Cambrick') and Lord Hawkesbury (Foreign Secretary) brings up a French commode or 'cacking' chair (note the pan of 'French Pap' which Britannia is being fed).

The Nursery – With Britannia Reposing in Peace
James Gillray, 2 December 1802

An 'Incroyable'
Carle Vernet, c.1810

**Talma Giving Napoleon a Lesson in
Deportment and Imperial Dignity**
French print, 1813

The brief period of peace also gave the rest of the world a chance to see the latest Paris fashions. Amongst these were the clothes worn by male dandies known as 'Les Incroyables' (The Incredibles) which included baggy trousers, high-collared coats and large cravats, made fun of here (*above left*) by the French artist Carle Vernet (1758-1836). Gillray later mocked the French fashion for high collars and in 'Les Invisibles' (*right*) makes them so large that they almost hide people's faces altogether. Bonaparte himself was not without a sense of fashion and in the anonymous French print (*above right*) from 1813 he is shown being given lessons in deportment by the famous French actor François-Joseph Talma.

Les Invisibles
James Gillray, 1810

1803

T HE FRAGILE PEACE that had followed the signing of the Treaty of Amiens was finally broken when Britain declared war on France in May 1803. The French government had been angered by Britain's reluctance to abandon the island of Malta – its only naval base in the Mediterranean – as agreed by the treaty, and Britain also felt that the French had breached its terms by annexing neutral Switzerland and a number of Italian states. France's immediate reaction was to annexe the German state of Hanover, of which George III was Elector, arrest all British citizens in France aged 18-60 as prisoners-of-war, and begin to amass in Boulogne a huge invasion force known as the 'Army of England' under the personal command of Napoleon. Britain responded by capturing a number of French islands in the West Indies, including St Lucia and Tobago, and making raids on the French coast at Dieppe and Calais. The propaganda war also began to escalate and this year saw James Gillray's creation of the tiny cartoon character 'Little Boney' to portray Napoleon.

German Nonchalence [*sic*], or the Vexation of Little Boney
vide the Diplomatique's Late Journey through Paris
James Gillray, 1 January 1803

Maniac-Ravings, or Little Boney in a Strong Fit
James Gillray, 24 May 1803

Bonaparte was well known for his fits of rage. 'German Nonchalence' (*opposite*) has the added interest that it is the first ever drawing to feature the First Consul as the character 'Little Boney'. The allusion is to the fact that, to Bonaparte's annoyance, the new Austrian Envoy Extraordinary (ambassador or *diplomatique*) to Britain drove past the Tuileries Palace en route to London without stopping to pay his respects. (Gillray has him nonchalantly taking snuff as he passes by.) The second drawing (*above*) records the extraordinary outburst made by Bonaparte at the British ambassador, Lord Whitworth, during a public reception at the Tuileries Palace on 13 March 1803 and reported in his official despatch to London the following day. Later the same year, at another reception, the First Consul became embroiled in a dispute with the Russian Ambassador, Markov. The artist here portrays the ambassador as a giant Cossack (*right*), personifying Russia, about to punch the tiny Napoleon.

A Tit Bit for a Russian Ambassador!!!
British print, June 1803

Armed Heroes – *vide Military Appearances at St Stephen's & at St Cloud's on Ye Day of Defiance*
James Gillray, 18 May 1803

A Stoppage to a Stride Over the Globe
British print, 16 April 1803

After one year and 16 days of peace, war was declared between Britain and France on 18 May 1803. In 'Armed Heroes' (*above*), published on that day, a defiant but terrified Prime Minister Lord Addington appears dressed in military uniform astride a plate of the Roast Beef of Old England. Behind him sits a dejected Lord Hawkesbury (Foreign Secretary) while across the Channel an aggressive but small Bonaparte draws his sword. The cartoon also refers to Addington's speech to Parliament (St Stephen's) two days earlier when, dressed in military uniform (which led to ridicule by some), he announced that negotiations had broken down. (St Cloud's is a reference to the French Parliament.) 'A Stoppage' (*left*), meanwhile, has a massive Bonaparte sitting astride the globe with one foot on Switzerland and the other on Italy while being threatened by a tiny John Bull who hacks at his left foot with a sword. (This latter image was very popular and was reprinted in May 1806 and January 1807).

The Oak and The Mushroom
British print, May 1803

An English Bull Dog and a Corsican Blood Hound
British print, August 1803

The general mood of British defiance is also shown in these three cartoons, with Jack Tar (the symbolic British sailor) defending the English oak against Bonaparte in the guise of a giant mushroom (*above left*), the English Bull Dog (*above right*) devouring the bloodhound Bonaparte (this cartoon was reissued in 1815), and (*right*) Jack Tar astride a whale (representing the Royal Navy) swallowing up Napoleon in an allusion to the Bible story of Jonah.

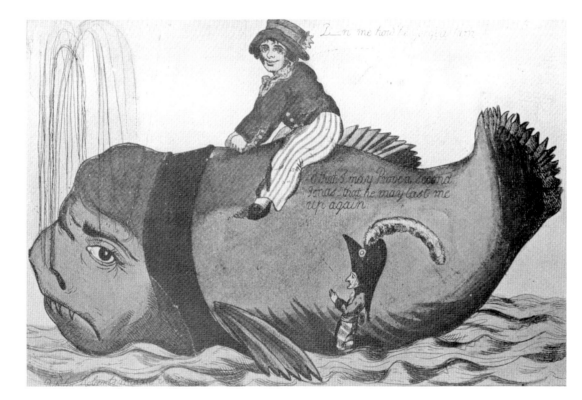

Little Boney in the Whale's Belly
British print, 1803

John Bull Teazed by an Ear-Wig!!
Temple West, 6 April 1803

One of the main issues affecting the peace was Britain's refusal to evacuate Malta – the key naval base for the Mediterranean – without guarantees which Bonaparte was unable to give. Occupied by Napoleon en route to the French invasion of Egypt it was subsequently taken by Britain.

In the drawing (*left*) by Temple West (fl. 1803-4) a huge John Bull is shown eating his bread (Ceylon, another disputed British territory) and cheese (Malta) while being pestered by a tiny Bonaparte earwig. The French print (*below*) has Pitt pulling the strings of his puppet Addington while a jester (standing on the Treaty of Amiens) cracks a jug in the form of George III on the rocky island of Malta.

The Pitcher Goes So Often to the Well That at Last It Breaks
French print, 1803

The Bone of Contention, or the English Bull Dog and the Corsican Monkey
Charles Ansell, 14 June 1803

In 'The Bone of Contention' (*above*) by Charles Ansell (Charles Williams, fl.1797-1830) the bone is Malta, with the British Bulldog urinating on Bonaparte's threatened invasion fleet. Meanwhile, in 'Green Spectacles' (*right*) the jealous, green-eyed First Consul, seated on a rock labelled 'Usurped Power', gazes enviously not only at Malta and British possessions in the West Indies and Egypt but also at Britain itself.

Green Spectacles, or Consular Goggles!!
British print, June 1803

John Bull Clipping the Corsican's Wings!!
British print, September 1803

The perceived imminent threat of French invasion led to a new call for soldiers in Britain. The militia, by now 80,000 strong, were called out on 25 March 1803 and on 28 June the House of Commons agreed to raise the regular army from 130,000 to 180,000. By the autumn of 1803, nearly 350,000 men had also joined volunteer regiments. This time the new recruits were no longer treated with derision by the caricaturists and the general mood of 'Britain can take it' was reflected in a wealth of morale-boosting prints which appeared at this time, as well as popular anti-French songs such as 'Britons, Strike Home!'

Facing the Enemy
Isaac Cruikshank, 1 October 1803

John Bull Sounding His Bugle!!
George Woodward, November 1803

Hop, Step and Jump
British print, 1 January 1801

Johnny Bull Giving Boney a Pull
Isaac Cruikshank, 7 August 1803

*It's cursed heavy!
I wish it had been Malta!*

*What thee hast got it hast thee? — the Devil do thee
good with it   Old Measter Chatham used to say
it was a Millstone about my Neck —, so perhaps
I may feel more lightsome without it.*

Boney in Possession of the Millstone
Charles Ansell, 5 July 1803

The first major military action by the French after the declaration of war was to invade the north German state of Hanover in June, which was particularly poignant for Britain as George III's family had been Electors (rulers) of Hanover for generations.

In Ansell's cartoon (*left*) the artist quotes Pitt's view that Hanover had long been a millstone around Britain's neck and puts it literally around Bonaparte's neck. The French cartoon (*below*) has General Edouard Mortier, later one of Napoleon's first marshals, vanquishing John Bull (note cricket bat and beer) while holding the deeds of Hanover in his hand.

The Quarrel
French print, 1803

In Gillray's famous drawing (*right*), featuring George III and a tiny Napoleon, the allusion is to Jonathan Swift's satire *Gulliver's Travels* (1726) where Gulliver visits Brobdingnag, a land of giants. (Apparently when George III saw this drawing he declared it inaccurate as it shows him wearing a bag wig with a military uniform.) 'The Corsican Pest' (*below*), meanwhile, has Beelzebub, 'the prince of devils', dressed as a French Republican in a *bonnet rouge* and tricolour sash, toasting Bonaparte for his dinner. He sits in a guillotine chair beneath which lie the skulls of the early revolutionary leaders Maximilien Robespierre and Jean-Paul Marat.

The King of Brobdingnag and Gulliver –
vide Swift's Gulliver's Voyage to Brobdingnag
James Gillray, 26 June 1803

The Corsican Pest, or Belzebub Going to Supper
James Gillray, 6 October 1803

Boney and Talley – The Corsican Carcase-Butcher's Reckoning Day
James Gillray, September 1803

With large parts of Europe under his control, Napoleon finally decided to invade Britain and began to assemble large numbers of troops along the Channel coast of France. In 'Boney and Talley' (*above*), Talleyrand – who was against the invasion – tries to prevent Bonaparte from foolishly rushing out of his butcher's shop (note the carcasses of conquered countries) to attack the huge British Bull, surrounded by sea and the Royal Navy, especially as the Russian bear has put its head around the door (hinting at the possibility of Russia forming an alliance with Britain). A similar theme appears in 'Selling the Skin' (*opposite top*) – with Britannia about to ring a bell marked 'British Valour'. And Bonaparte is weighed and found wanting in the other cartoon featuring Britannia (*opposite bottom left*). Meanwhile, Cruikshank's 'Dreadful Fears of Invasion' (*opposite bottom right*) adumbrates a cartoon from the Second World War by Pont (Graham Laidler) nearly 140 years later, which equally portrays the average Briton as being completely unperturbed by the threat of invasion.

Selling the Skin Before the Bear is Caught, or Cutting up the Bull Before He is Killed
Isaac Cruikshank, 24 December 1803

**Britannia Weighing the Fate of Europe,
or John Bull Too Heavy for Buonaparte**
British print, December 1803

Dreadful Fears of Invasion!!
Isaac Cruikshank, 2 December 1803

57

The Hand-Writing upon the Wall
James Gillray, 24 August 1803

Consular Games

The Game of Brag   **The Game of Hazard**

George Woodward, 1803

As the French continued to build up their forces in Boulogne and elsewhere the flow of propaganda cartoons increased. In Gillray's drawing (*top*) alluding to the Old Testament story of Belshazzar's Feast, Bonaparte sits next to a huge Josephine, behind whom stand his three sisters. On the table are the British dishes that Bonaparte hopes soon to devour – including St James's (George III's London palace) and the Bank of England. One of Jehovah's hands appears from the clouds and points to the words indicating that Bonaparte's time is up while the other holds a balance in which a royal crown outweighs 'Despotism'. Bonaparte looks up alarmed, as do the three Grenadier Guards behind him.

Two French views of the projected invasion across the English Channel. In 'A Contrary Wind' (*top*) a British soldier hides behind the skirts of British women who are trying to blow the French invasion fleet back with their fans. One woman says to him: 'Quick! Hide yourself. They are here.' Meanwhile, 'Save What You Can!' (*bottom*) has Britons trying to escape with whole cities piled onto stretchers before the invaders arrive.

A Contrary Wind – Valiant Efforts by the English Fair Sex to Impede the Invasion
French print, c.1803

Save What You Can!
French print, c.1803

1804

I N FEBRUARY 1804 a plot to assassinate Bonaparte by British-backed French monarchists – the so-called Cadoudal Conspiracy – led to the execution of the Bourbon Duc d'Enghien, an act which received international condemnation and the breaking of diplomatic ties between Russia and France. It also resulted, in December that year, in Bonaparte crowning himself Napoleon I, hereditary Emperor of France, to assure the rule of his dynasty. For many this was against all the principles of republicanism for which the French Revolution had been fought and much overseas support for him began to fall away – Beethoven even tore up the dedication to Napoleon of his *Eroica Symphony*. This year Napoleon also created the elite Imperial Guard, revived the pre-Revolutionary military title Marshal (appointing 18 senior generals to the rank), and instituted a new award for valour, the Légion d'Honneur.

Meanwhile in Britain, the year began with continued anxiety about the possibility of a French invasion. Addington resigned as Prime Minister, leading to the return in May – to the relief of many – of the pro-war Pitt. (As Canning wrote: 'Pitt is to Addington /As London is to Paddington.') At about the same time, the Royal Navy hit back at France's allies, taking the Dutch island of Surinam in the West Indies – using the new British invention of shrapnel artillery shells – and later in the year, capturing a Spanish treasure fleet (Spain declared war on Britain on 14 December).

Dutch Embarkation, or Needs Must When the Devil Drives!!!
George Woodward, January 1804

The King of Brobdingnag and Gulliver
James Gillray, 10 February 1804

French print, c.May 1804

On 2 January 1804 Bonaparte reviewed the French invasion fleet at Boulogne and still believed that – with a few clear days and a good wind – he could cross the Channel and conquer Britain, which he described as 'the modern Carthage' (the Roman Empire's ancient foe). However, he also knew that without command of the sea this would be impossible, and the British public had great and justifiable confidence in the might of the Royal Navy.

In Gillray's second famous cartoon (*top*) featuring George III as the King of Brobdingnag (see also p.55) from Jonathan Swift's *Gulliver's Travels* (1726), Bonaparte is the tiny Gulliver trying to sail across a cistern to the amusement of the king, Queen Charlotte

and various other members of the British royal family (as well as two Beefeater guards). This print appeared in many forms and a Spanish version was popular during the Peninsular War. The drawing (*opposite*) by George Moutard Woodward (1760-1809) – also known as 'Mustard George' – shows unhappy Dutchmen (who have been 'liberated' by France) being forced into walnut-shell gunboats to attack Britain. Meanwhile, the French cartoon (*above*) shows new Prime Minister William Pitt – appointed in May – sitting on George III's shoulders and hiding behind a rock, trying to discover from which direction the French squadrons will attack.

In early 1804 the Chouan (Royalist) leader Georges Cadoudal – who had led an uprising against the French Revolutionary government in 1799 and had been implicated in the plot to blow up Bonaparte on the Rue Nicaise in Paris in December 1800 (see p.39) – hatched a conspiracy to assassinate the First Consul. With around 50 others – including General Charles Pichegru (a hero of the early Revolutionary Wars) – he planned to kill Bonaparte during a parade at the Place du Carrousel in Paris. However the plot was discovered and Cadoudal was arrested on 13 February. Believing that the conspirators intended to put a Bourbon back on the throne, Bonaparte chose to believe (completely erroneously) that this would be Louis Antoine de Bourbon-Condé, Duc d'Enghien. The only son of the Prince de Condé (a descendant of the Bourbon king Louis II), d'Enghien had been living in the German city of Etterheim in the neutral duchy of Baden, near the French border, since the Peace of Lunéville in 1801. In order to arrest him Republican forces had to cross illegally into neutral country and kidnap him. After being taken to the prison at Vincennes, Paris, he was summarily tried and shot in March. Pichegru was murdered while in prison in April and Cadoudal was guillotined on 25 June.

The French cartoon (*right*) shows Napoleon's security chief, General Savary, in despair after being held responsible for the execution of d'Enghien.

French print, 1804

The Right Owner
Isaac Cruikshank, 1 June 1804

Seeing his position at risk from Royalist assassination plots, Bonaparte decided that – despite his Republican background – he should be made hereditary Emperor of France, thereby establishing a dynasty with the right of succession for his future children to rule France after his death. In May 1804 the French Senate approved the title of 'Emperor' and Bonaparte thereafter became known as Napoleon I.

Needless to say, Napoleon – who had once declared: 'I am the Revolution' – immediately became the target of satirical prints, including a number alluding to the 'true' royal ruler of France, the guillotined Louis XVI. 'The Right Owner' (*above*) has the ghost of Louis claiming his crown back.

**The Grand Coronation Procession of Napoleone I, Emperor of France,
from the Church of Notre Dame, December 2, 1804**
James Gillray, 27 December 1804

On 2 December 1804 Napoleon I crowned himself and his wife at the cathedral of Notre Dame in Paris in the presence of Pope Pius VII. The ceremony and attendant processions were conducted with great pomp and were widely lampooned. The drawings by Gillray and George Cruikshank (*above and right*) are fairly good-natured but the German cartoon (*bottom*) by Jean-Frédéric Clar (fl.1800s) has Napoleon's throne built on layers of bodies and skulls.

George Cruikshank in William Combe, *The Life of Napoleon* (1815)

The Emperor Napoleon
Jean-Frédéric Clar, 1805

63

1805

THIS YEAR SAW peace proposals by Napoleon to Pitt in January which, once rejected, led to the final preparations for an invasion of Britain. Meanwhile, there were further French gains in the Italian peninsula with the annexation of Genoa, the transformation of the Italian Republic into a royal state and the coronation of Napoleon as King of Italy. On 11 April 1805 Austria, Sweden, Britain, Russia and a number of German states formed the Third Coalition and declared war against France. As a result, Napoleon abandoned his plans for the invasion of England, formed a new Grand Army and moved his forces east. When Austrian forces under General Mack von Leiberich invaded French-occupied Bavaria Napoleon counter-attacked and in October he surrounded and captured Mack's entire army at Ulm. He then drove on into Austria itself to occupy Vienna and then marched north and smashed the Russians and the Austrians at the Battle of Austerlitz (also known as the Battle of the Three Emperors), giving the French almost complete domination on land in western Europe. Beaten, the Austrians signed the Treaty of Pressburg in December and the Russians withdrew. Meanwhile, by contrast, in a major battle which finally ended Napoleon's ambitions at sea, the British under Admiral Nelson destroyed the Franco-Spanish fleet at Trafalgar near Cadiz off the Mediterranean coast of Spain. Also on the last day of 1805, Napoleon made a final split with the French Revolution by abandoning the Republican calendar and adopting the more common Gregorian calendar.

The Plumb-Pudding in Danger, or State Epicures taking *un petit souper*
James Gillray, 26 February 1805

In January 1805 Napoleon made peace overtures to George III in which he suggested that Britain and France could divide the world between them. 'The Plumb-Pudding in Danger' (*above*) has Pitt (left) in military uniform, with a three-pronged fork representing a trident – the symbol of naval power – slicing off a large piece of ocean from the plum pudding that is the globe. 'Little Boney', meanwhile, uses his sword to cut off most of the European mainland.

With the possibility of invasion still a real threat, Britain braced itself. On 2 August Napoleon returned from Italy and set off for Boulogne where 90,000 troops and 2000 boats had assembled. From here he wrote to the Empress Josephine: 'Let me be master of the Straits for six hours and we shall be masters of the world.' For him the English Channel was 'a ditch which will be leaped whenever one has the boldness to try' and it seemed that he was finally about to try. Meanwhile, his advances into Italy had also begun to concern the other major European powers. The Anglo-Russian Treaty had been ratified in July and by October Austria and Prussia looked likely to join a Third Coalition against France.

In Gillray's cartoon (*right*), George III – as England's patron saint, St George (and dressed in the uniform of his own regiment, 'the Blues' or Royal Horse Guards) – comes to the rescue of Britannia who is being attacked by the dragon Napoleon. Charles Ansell, meanwhile (*below*), depicts the Austrian double-headed eagle, the Russian bear and the Prussian boar attacking Napoleon (as the tiny Tom Thumb of the nursery tale and dressed in his coronation robes) from the east while the British lion, already in France, does so from the west. In the background are armed rats, representing German states willing to lend a hand, and in the centre a Spaniard, a Dutchman and a Swiss are taking off the yokes around their necks (though in reality it would be some considerable time before they would be able to do so). The anticipated positions of the Allies in this drawing would also soon prove to be illusory.

St George and the Dragon – a Design for an Equestrian Statue, from the Original in Windsor Castle
James Gillray, 2 August 1805

Tom Thumb at Bay, or the Sovereigns of the Forest Roused at Last!!
Charles Ansell, October 1805

An English Set-To or British Tars Clearing the Deck of the *Téméraire* of French and Spaniards
British print, 1805

With the renewal of war in 1803 Vice-Admiral Nelson was given command of
the Royal Navy in the Mediterranean. On 30 March 1805 the French Fleet
under Vice-Admiral Pierre-Charles Villeneuve broke out of the French port
of Toulon with a view to sailing to the West Indies, leading the Royal Navy
away from Europe and then returning rapidly to join with the Spanish Fleet
to clear the English Channel in preparation for Napoleon's invasion of
Britain. However, this tactic did not work and Villeneuve eventually
returned to the main Spanish Mediterranean port of Cadiz. He then led a
combined Franco-Spanish fleet of 33 ships-of-the-line out of Cadiz and
encountered Nelson's force just off Cape Trafalgar. At the Battle of Trafalgar
(21 October 1805) the Royal Navy comprehensively defeated the Franco-
Spanish fleet and Villeneuve was taken prisoner when his flagship
Bucentaure surrendered (he later committed suicide). However, a major
loss during the battle was the death of Nelson after a musketball fired from
the French ship *Redoubtable* shattered his spine while he was standing in
full uniform on the quarter-deck of his flagship, HMS *Victory*. His body was
later returned to London where it lay in state in St Paul's Cathedral.

The Death of Admiral Lord Nelson in the Moment of Victory!
James Gillray, 23 December 1805

'An English Set-To' (*opposite*) gives an impression of hand-to-hand fighting on the deck of the British ship HMS *Téméraire* during the Battle of Trafalgar, while Gillray's cartoon (*above*) pays tribute to the nation's most famous admiral. 'The Sailor's Monument' (*right*) by contrast, criticises the British Government's decision to make sailors pay to see the tomb of Nelson in St Paul's Cathedral. It shows a typical Jack Tar who has made his own memorial.

**The Sailor's Monument –
to the Memory of Lord Nelson**
George Woodward, December 1805

**The Surrender of Ulm, or Buonaparte and
General Mack Coming to a Right Understanding**
James Gillray, 6 November 1805

**Boney Beating Mack, and Nelson Giving him a Whack!!, or the British Tars Giving
Boney His Heart's Desire: Ships, Colonies and Commerce**
George Cruikshank, 19 November 1805

After the formation of the Third Coalition, Napoleon abandoned his plans to invade Britain and on 27 August marched his Grand Army from Boulogne and across the Rhine to try and defeat the Austrian forces before they could be joined by the Russian Army. Baron Karl Mack von Leiberich, in charge of the Austrian Army, invaded pro-French Bavaria on 3 September and concentrated his forces at Ulm in the German principality of Württemberg on the upper Danube near Stuttgart. Here he was surrounded and on 20 October 1805 was forced to capitulate with 27,000 men – some of the best troops in Europe – at almost no cost to Napoleon.

In Gillray's cartoon (*top*) General Mack is seen prostrate before Napoleon to whom he presents his sword and the keys to the huge fortress of Ulm (seen behind). The subtitle reads: 'Intended as a Specimen of French Victories, i.e. Conquering Without Bloodshed.' There is also a strong suggestion that Mack has been bribed into surrender by the French. 'Boney Beating Mack' (*above*) is the first cartoon attributed to George Cruikshank (1792-1878), son of Isaac Cruikshank and then aged 13. In this Mack kneels to Napoleon whose words allude to the actual speech he made to the Austrian General on the surrender of Ulm: 'I desire nothing further upon the Continent; I want ships, colonies and commerce.' Meanwhile, in the background, Admiral Nelson presents Britannia with the battered ships of the combined French and Spanish fleets he has just defeated at Trafalgar.

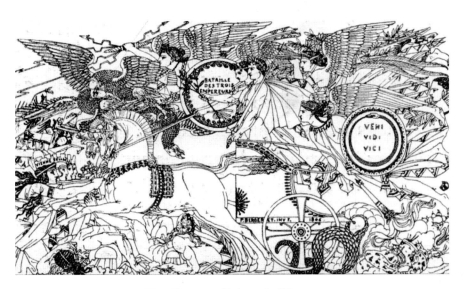

The Emperor Driven by Victory
French print, 30 September 1806

After the Battle of Ulm the route to Vienna was open to Napoleon.
The Austrians decided not to defend the city and thus the French
marched in and Napoleon himself took up residence at the
Schönbrunn Palace. However, he did not remain in the city for long
and, leaving a garrison of 20,000, decided to engage the Allies to the
north of Vienna near the village of Austerlitz (now Slavkov) close to
Brunn (Brno) in Moravia in what is now the Czech Republic. Also
known as the Battle of the Three Emperors, because the rulers of
France, Austria and Russia were all present, the Battle of Austerlitz
was fought on 2 December 1805. The result was a resounding victory
for Napoleon – the Allies suffered 16,000 killed and wounded and
more than 11,000 taken prisoner, while French casualties were only
1800 killed or captured and 6800 wounded. The Russian casualties
(11,000) were particularly bad with two of the country's finest
regiments almost completely destroyed. The Battle of Austerlitz also
put an end to the Third Coalition, which Austria left to sign the
Peace of Pressburg on 26 December 1805. To celebrate the
tremendous victory at Austerlitz – which left France masters of
Europe on land – Napoleon built the Arc de Triomphe and erected
the victory column (with a statue of himself on top) in the Place
Vendôme in Paris.

1806

A MAJOR BLOW to the British in January 1806 was the sudden death, aged 46, of Prime Minister William Pitt. He was succeeded by his cousin Lord Grenville who led a 'Ministry of all the Talents' with Fox as Foreign Secretary. With its army still confined to its homeland, the Royal Navy was Britain's only weapon against the French Empire and its allies, and the year began well with the taking of the Dutch-held Cape of Good Hope at the tip of Africa which commanded the sea-route to the Orient (the Suez Canal had not yet been built). Then came the capture of the Italian island of Capri, followed by a popular uprising in nearby Calabria and a victory at Maida on the Italian mainland in July. At about the same time a British force briefly took the Spanish colony of Buenos Aires in what is now Argentina, leading to the hope of beating the Spanish across South America.

Meanwhile, Napoleon began to install his family as rulers of France's puppet states. The Batavian Republic now became the Kingdom of Holland with Louis Bonaparte as its monarch, and Joseph Bonaparte was created King of Naples. In July Napoleon also began to consolidate the conquered German states as the Confederation of the Rhine and later abolished the 1000-year-old Holy Roman Empire, leading its ruler, Francis II, to retitle himself Francis I of Austria. Prussia was unhappy with these developments and in October joined with Britain and Russia in a Fourth Coalition and declared war on France. However, after joint Prussian-Saxon armies under the Duke of Brunswick were defeated near Erfurt at two battles which took place on the same day – at Jena and Auerstädt – they sued for peace. Napoleon then entered Potsdam to visit the tomb of Frederick the Great and marched his troops through Berlin's Brandenburg Gate. In November he pronounced his famous Berlin Decrees which introduced the Continental System whereby it was intended that the whole of occupied Europe would blockade Britain into submission. Soon afterwards he marched his forces further east into Russian-held Poland, occupying Warsaw and then being halted briefly north of the capital by the Russians at the indecisive battles of Pultusk and Golymin, which both took place of 26 December.

The Death of Pitt
French print, 1806

William Pitt, who had been prime minister of Britain for 19 years, died on 23 January 1806. These drawings show opposing views of Pitt's death from the British and French sides. The first French drawing (*opposite*) has Pitt being carried down to Hell by the Devil, snapping the strings by which he has led a blind George III. The king himself falls into an abyss over a sack marked 'Depot of the Crimes of the English Government' while a Frenchman holds up a scroll on which are written 'Victory of Austerlitz' and 'Continental Peace'. In the second French cartoon (*far right*) the architect of the Third Coalition – holding a despatch box labelled 'Coalitions' and with his feet on a torn-up Treaty of Amiens and a box marked 'Rights of Nations' – is confronted by Napoleon, whose sword has the inscription 'Austerlitz'. By contrast the British caricature (*right*) shows Pitt as an evergreen figure (note the guillotine and gallows in the background).

'The Honeymoon' (*below*) celebrates the new British government'. It shows Fox dancing with Britannia – with music supplied by Sheridan (on fiddle) and Lord Derby – while George III looks on.

An Ever Green!!
British print, 3 April 1806

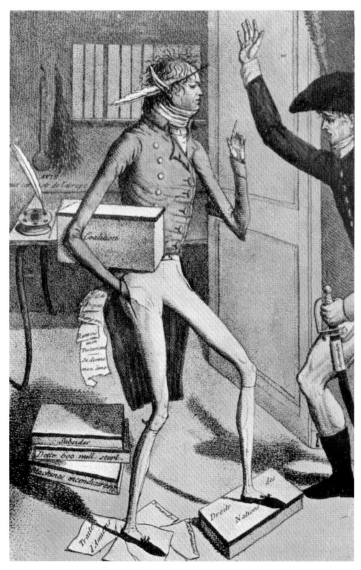

Pitt, Pitiable and Spited
French print, 1806

The Honey Moon
British print, February 1806

French print, 1806

**'Prussians! It is not enough
to win – I want <u>blood</u>!'**
French print, 1806

Threatened by Napoleon's consolidation of many of the German states into the Confederation of the Rhine and the abolition of the 1000-year-old Holy Roman Empire, Prussia and Saxony joined Britain and Russia in a Fourth Coalition against France in October 1806. King Frederick William III of Prussia had been encouraged in this move by his dominant wife, Queen Louise. However, before the Russian Army could come to their aid, Napoleon's forces attacked. Near the towns of Jena and Auerstädt, 25 miles east of Erfurt, Napoleon's army met the Prussians and Saxons under Karl William Ferdinand, Duke of Brunswick (brother-in-law of George III and father-in-law of the Prince of Wales). At the Battle of Jena-Auerstädt on 14 October 1806, the French won a decisive victory. The Prussians and Saxons lost about 36,000 killed or wounded – including 20 generals and the Duke of Brunswick himself. French losses were around 4000. Britain now seemed to be alone. As the British poet William Wordsworth said (in 'November 1806'):

> Another year! – another deadly blow!
> Another mighty empire overthrown!
> And we are left, or shall be left, alone;
> The last that dare to struggle with the foe.

Precipitate March of the Russian Army Flying to the Aid of the Prussians
French print, 1806

The French cartoon (*top left*) shows the plight of the King and Queen of Prussia. Frederick William is asking Louise where she is dragging him as the queen pulls him further into a bog in which the Prince of Hesse (right) has already sunk up to his neck. To the left Tsar Alexander I of Russia fears the same thing will happen to him. The second French drawing (*top right*) is a portrait of Queen Louise seated side-saddle on a wooden horse. Behind her sits a devil, who is using a speaking tube to project his words through her mouth. The third cartoon (*above*) satirises the slowness of the Russian forces who are unable to arrive in time to help (note that the Prussian king is being carried off by a French eagle as the Russians, mounted on a lobster and two tortoises, amble slowly along).

The Battle of Pul-Tusk
British print, 1807

After the Battle of Jena-Auerstädt, the French pressed on to the east, entering Poland in November and occupying Warsaw on 18 December. Marshal Jean Lannes then fought the Russians under General Count Bennigsen (one of the conspirators in the assassination of Tsar Paul) in the Polish town of Pultusk, 32 miles north of Warsaw. The Battle of Pultusk (26 December 1806) was indecisive but the Russians were forced to retreat.

In this British cartoon (*above*), the French are drawn as apes, their Polish allies as literally poles and the Russians as bears led by a barrel labelled 'Spirited Benn-in-Gin' (a pun on Bennigsen). Napoleon, swinging from a tree, says: 'I am determined to beat those brutes, in spite of their teeth' and hence the title of the cartoon, punning on the town's name (note that the French apes all have pincers to pull the bears' teeth or tusks).

**Tiddy Doll, the Great French Gingerbread-Baker, Drawing Out a New Batch of Kings –
His Man, Hopping Tally, Mixing up the Dough**
James Gillray, 23 January 1806

A Mediterranean Clan Connection
French print, c.1810

In 1806 Napoleon created a number of new kingdoms including Bavaria, Württemberg, Baden and Saxony. He also gave royal appointments to his own brothers. On 30 March 1806 Joseph became King of Naples and on 5 June Louis became King of Holland (later, on 7 July 1807, Jerome became King of Westphalia). However, his brother Lucien – who had been President of the Council of Five Hundred and had helped Napoleon come to power – refused a royal title as this would only be on condition that he gave up his wife. (Lucien later tried to sail for the USA but was captured by the British and spent the rest of the war on an estate near Ludlow, Shropshire.)

Gillray's famous cartoon (*above left*), published on the day of Pitt's death, features Napoleon in the guise of Tiddy Doll, a famous itinerant London gingerbread-maker from the reign of George II. His real name unknown, he gained his pseudonym from the chant he sang while serving his customers – its refrain was 'Tiddy-doll-lol-lol'. In the cartoon Napoleon can be seen pulling out three new kings – Bavaria, Württemberg and Baden. Already in the basket (left) are Bonaparte family members – 'True Corsican Kinglings for Home Consumption & Exportation'. In the background can be seen his assistant Talleyrand ('hopping' referring to his club foot) at the 'Political Kneading Trough', about to hand Turkey, Poland and Hungary to the baker. The anonymous French drawing (*left*) has the Bonaparte clan striding the globe. They are (left to right) Jerome, Lucien, Napoleon, Louis and Joseph.

News from Calabria! Capture of Buenos Ayres!,
i.e. the Comforts of an Imperial *Dejeune* at St Clouds
James Gillray, 18 September 1806

The imposition of the Bonaparte family as rulers of foreign countries led to a number of rebellions. Notable amongst these was a peasant revolt in Calabria (the 'toe' of southern Italy), which followed the deposition of the King of Naples and his replacement with Napoleon's older brother Joseph. To support the uprising Britain sent more than 5000 troops from its base in Sicily together with a number of guns. The Battle of Maida (6 July 1806) – after which Maida Vale in London is named – resulted in 500 French killed and 1100 taken prisoner for the loss of 45 British (plus 280 wounded). After the major defeats of the Allies in

Europe in 1805 this, together with the (albeit brief) capture of Buenos Aires in Argentina from the Spanish on 27 June, was greeted with much enthusiasm in Britain.

In Gillray's cartoon (*above*), Napoleon is seen greatly agitated by the Allied victories. He not only pulls the ear of Talleyrand (who has brought the news) but also tries to hit him with a tea-urn in the shape of the world. However, as he does so the contents pour into the lap of Josephine. Other messengers bring news of uprisings in Germany, Italy, Sicily and other parts of Napoleon's empire.

LORD GRENVILLE'S 'Ministry of all the Talents' collapsed in March 1807 over the question of Catholic Emancipation (to which George III was strongly opposed) and was replaced by a Tory government led by the Duke of Portland. On the war front, cut off from Europe by the blockade which Napoleon called the 'Continental System', Britain looked further afield to attack France and its allies. British troops seized Spanish-ruled Montevideo, capital of what was then Banda Oriental (now Uruguay), took and lost Buenos Aires again and sent an unsuccessful expedition to Egypt which, after capturing Alexandria, returned to England. An abortive raid was also made on the Dardanelles as a show of strength against France's new ally, Turkey.

Napoleon, meanwhile, continued to steamroller his way across eastern Europe, annexing Swedish Pomerania in January and fighting a bloody battle against Russian and Prussian troops at Eylau (Bagrationovsk) in East Prussia – near the important seaport of Königsberg (Kaliningrad) – the following month. He then took Danzig (Gdansk) after a long siege and, following a stalemate at the Battle of Heilsberg in June, hammered the Russians at Friedland (Pravdinsk) and marched on to occupy Königsberg itself. By the subsequent Treaty of Tilsit, famously signed after a meeting between Napoleon and Tsar Alexander I on a raft in the middle of the River Niemen (which marked the Russian border), the Fourth Coalition was effectively over and Britain was left to face the French alone.

Napoleon now ruled over the biggest empire in Europe's history – stretching from the Pyrenees to the River Vistula and from the Baltic coast to the Ionian Sea – and with an army potentially numbering almost five million. With only the Royal Navy as its effective defence, Britain was determined that the Danish Fleet should not fall into French hands as a result of the Treaty of Tilsit. Thus British and Hanoverian troops besieged Copenhagen until the Danes surrendered and handed over their ships. In October France declared war on Britain's only remaining ally, Portugal, and crossed Spain to invade the country soon afterwards.

The Giant Commerce Overwhelming the Pigmy Blockade
George Woodward, 27 January 1807

The 'Continental System', which Napoleon had first introduced in his Berlin Decrees of November 1806, quickly began to bite, with all the major ports of French-occupied Europe denied to Britain. However, the blockade soon became a two-way process – the Royal Navy denying Europe sugar, cotton and coffee from the USA and the West Indies, and pepper and other spices from India.

In these three cartoons, Britain is seen to prosper despite the blockade while Napoleon and France suffer. In Woodward's drawing (*opposite*) the figure of the giant Commerce is made of British export goods such as wool, leather, calico, porcelain, steel and gin ('Maidstone's Geneva') – all of which were now denied the French and the occupied countries of mainland Europe. Ansell's 'The English Lamb and the French Tiger' (*right*) has a skinny Napoleon drinking a thin gruel while the celebrated giant Daniel Lambert (representing Britain) tucks into a huge piece of roast beef. (Daniel Lambert was the former keeper of Leicester prison and from 1806 to 1807 was one of the sights of London – when he died in 1809 he weighed nearly 53 stone.) By contrast, the French drawing (*below*) has George III (right) about to fall off his chair in despair when he learns of the effects of the blockade on Britain.

The English Lamb and the French Tiger
Charles Ansell, April 1806

**George III and His Ministers in Despair Over the Effects
of the Continental Blockade in England**
French print, c.1807

The Political Cock-Horse
George Sauley, 10 March 1807

In an attempt to halt Napoleon's march eastwards, an Allied force
of 67,000 Russians and 10,000 Prussians under the command of
General Bennigsen attacked the French in a blizzard at Eylau in
East Prussia, 23 miles southeast of Königsberg (now Kaliningrad)
on the Baltic Sea. The bloody but indecisive Battle of Eylau
(7-8 February 1807) ended with the retreat of the Allied army and
the loss of 15,000 French killed or wounded and 10,000 prisoners
while the Allies lost 11,000 killed, 14,000 wounded and 3000
prisoners.

In the cartoon by the British artist George Sauley (fl.1803-8)
the Russian General Bennigsen is seen leaping onto the back of
Napoleon's horse – which has stumbled on a stone marked
'Insatiable Ambition' – grabbing the reins and throwing Napoleon
to the ground. As Napoleon goes flying – dropping his sword
labelled 'Oppression' (which is about to impale him) John Bull
applauds, saying: 'Bravo. Bravo, brave Russians. One home-stroke
more and goodbye to Master Boney!'

The Conquering Heroes Return
French print, 1807

The Imperial Embrace on the Raft, or Boney's New Drop
Charles Ansell, July 1807

After the Battle of Eylau Napoleon's forces captured Danzig (now Gdansk) on 26 May 1807 and defeated a Russian army under General Bennigsen at Friedland (now Pravdinsk), 27 miles southeast of Königsberg. The Battle of Friedland (14 June 1807) led to great loss of life for the Russians as they were pushed back into the River Alle, many drowning. French losses were 12,100, while the Russians lost 10,000. After the battle – which effectively ended the Fourth Coalition – the French occupied Königsberg (which had been evacuated by the Russians) and then, on 25 June, Napoleon met Tsar Alexander I of Russia on a specially made, elaborately decorated raft anchored in the centre of the River Niemen near Tilsit (now Sovetsk). This led to the Treaty of Tilsit (signed by Russia on 7 July and Prussia two days later).

In the French drawing (*above left*) victorious French troops are shown being welcomed back in Paris after the battle. A sour-faced old lady (left) raises her umbrella against the roses, laurels and cherubs that accompany the amorous greetings of the young couples. Ansell's cartoon (*above right*), meanwhile, depicts the meeting on the raft on the River Niemen – the Tsar has dropped his crown while King Frederick William III of Prussia has fallen into the water. The other French cartoon (*right*) has a French soldier forcing the Tsar to throw up a number of territories – notably the Crimea and Poland – with the hope that George III will do likewise soon (the labels coming out of George's mouth include Ceylon, Malta and Pondicherry in India). On the right King Frederick William of Prussia declares he has nothing more to give, while France's new ally Turkey (left) applauds the punishment.

Better Late Than Never!
French print, 1807

Bombardment of Copenhagen by the Royal Navy
German print, 1807

**British Tars Towing the Danish Fleet into Harbour:
the Broad-Bottom Leviathan Trying to Swamp Billy's Old Boat,
and the Little Corsican Tottering on the Clouds of Ambition**
James Gillray, 1 October 1807

Spectres Visiting John Bull
Charles Williams, 3 February 1808

After the Treaty of Tilsit the British were determined to prevent the Danish fleet from falling into French hands. Thus on 16 August 1807 Britain made a pre-emptive strike (without a declaration of war) on Copenhagen, sending 18,000 British and Hanoverian troops to lay siege to the neutral Danish capital. On 2 September 27 Royal Navy ships added their firepower to the bombardment of the city which capitulated four days later. The Danes then handed over their entire fleet of 18 ships which were subsequently sailed back to England. However, though successful, this action did not have universal support in Britain.

A German view of the bombardment (*top left*) is shown in a popular print. Meanwhile, in Gillray's cartoon (*centre*) Lord Liverpool (Home Secretary) and Lord Castlereagh (Secretary for War and the Colonies) are seen rowing the 'Billy Pitt' in an allusion to Pitt's robust attitude to Napoleon, with Foreign Secretary Canning at the prow. As they tow the Danish fleet into harbour in Sheerness (Kent) they are sprayed by a three-headed whale-like creature (the 'leviathan') which has the heads of the leaders of the former British Government (also known as the 'Broad-Bottomed Ministry'). These are Lord Howick (former Foreign Secretary), Lord St Vincent (former First Lord of the Admiralty) and Lord Grenville (former Prime Minister). The cold water (labelled 'Opposition Clamour', 'Detraction'; and 'Envy') they are spraying onto the rowing-boat indicates their displeasure at the naval action. However, to the right can be seen John Bull shouting 'Rule Britannia' while Napoleon (in the clouds) is horrified and drops his 'Project for Subjugating the Sea'. In the distance can be seen Copenhagen flying a British flag while the continent is in flames. Williams' cartoon (*bottom*) shows the ghosts of Fox, Pitt and Edmund Burke ordering John Bull to erase the 'Vote of Thanks Respecting the Expedition to Copenhagen' from his journal.

Boney Stark Mad, or More Ships, Colonies & Commerce
Isaac and George Cruikshank, 1 January 1808

When Portugal refused to cooperate with Napoleon's Continental System to blockade Britain, France declared war and decided to invade the country by land via Spain. On 17 October 1807 a French army of 24,000 men crossed the Pyrenees into Spain via the northern border route at Bayonne. A month later General Andoche Junot entered Portugal and captured Lisbon without firing a shot on 30 November. However, the Regent of Portugal – together with the state treasures and the Portuguese navy – had by then already left the capital for Brazil, with the aid of the Royal Navy. Though there were anti-French riots in Lisbon on 13 December these were quickly suppressed and, after disbanding the Portuguese army, Junot became Governor-General of Portugal.

In the cartoon by Isaac and George Cruikshank (*above*) – whose title alludes to the statement made by Napoleon after the equally bloodless capture of Ulm (see p.68) – Napoleon can be seen taking out his frustration on Talleyrand (note his club foot) as Admiral Sir Sidney Smith escorts the Portuguese royal family to safety en route to Brazil.

THE YEAR 1808 BEGAN with the Russian invasion of Finland (then Swedish) and the French occupation of Rome. Elsewhere Austria invaded Bavaria again but were once more beaten back (and Vienna was again occupied by the French), the island of Capri was retaken by the French and Marshal Murat succeeded Joseph Bonaparte as King of Naples. However, the main events of 1808 took place in the Iberian peninsula, resulting in a war on two fronts for Napoleon. In February, the French army seized key forts in northern Spain and the following month French troops entered Madrid. However, before long anti-French riots broke out in the capital, and when both King Charles IV of Spain and his son Ferdinand were forced to abdicate in favour of Joseph Bonaparte, a nationwide uprising followed. Though generally no match for the French, the Spanish won a major victory at Bailen in July and put up stiff resistance at the sieges of Saragossa, Valencia and elsewhere. Spain then signed a treaty of alliance with Britain and in August Lieutenant-General Arthur Wellesley (the future Duke of Wellington) landed a British expeditionary force in Portugal (bringing with him the first ever war correspondent). After defeating the French at Obidos and Roliça he inflicted a major blow against them at the Battle of Vimeiro, near Lisbon, on 21 August, which led to the Convention of Cintra by which 26,000 French troops were sent back to France on British ships. In November Sir John Moore then drove on into Spain itself. Meanwhile, Napoleon himself led a counterattack from the north and after beating the Spanish at the Battle of Somosierra (30 November), entered Madrid and restored his brother to the throne. He then cut off Moore's escape route to Portugal, leaving the British expeditionary force trapped.

Spanish print, c.1808

After the occupation of Portugal, French troops were garrisoned in key Spanish cities, with Spanish permission, from the Portuguese border to the French frontier at Bayonne in order to establish a line of communication to Portugal. However, on the pretext of settling disputes in the Spanish royal family, Napoleon then ordered the seizure of a number of forts in the north of Spain and on 24 March Marshal Joachim Murat marched into Madrid with 18,000 men. Spanish resistance to this was considerable and there were riots in Madrid on 2 May which were brutally suppressed. By the Conference of Bayonne (April-May 1808), King Charles IV of Spain and his son King Ferdinand VII were forced to surrender their crowns and Napoleon then installed his brother Joseph (formerly King of Naples) on the throne. This led to even greater rebellion by the Spanish nationwide and on 6 June the Supreme Junta (or provisional government) formally declared war on France.

The Spanish print (*opposite*) shows the new king, Joseph Bonaparte, riding a cucumber (*pepino* in Catalan means both 'cucumber' and 'stupid'), wearing a suit of tankards and holding a tray of drinks (an allusion to his reputation as a drunkard). Goya, meanwhile (*right*), depicts the French imperial eagle as a half-plucked vulture being driven off by Spanish patriots. In Rowlandson's 'The Corsican Tiger at Bay' (*below*), which was very popular and appeared in a Spanish edition, the Napoleon tiger (actually drawn as a leopard) – standing on royal Bourbon dogs – is attacked by patriotic Spanish greyhounds while John Bull (right) takes aim with a musket. Meanwhile, the enchained Russian bear and Austrian eagle (and a Dutch frog) think it is time that they too were rid of Napoleon.

The Carnivorous Vulture
Francisco Goya, from *The Disasters of War* (1863)

The Corsican Tiger at Bay
Thomas Rowlandson, 8 July 1808

The Spanish Bull-Fight, or the Corsican Matador in Danger
James Gillray, 11 July 1808

The French General Pierre Dupont de L'Etang –
in charge of pacifying the southern region of
Andalusia – sacked Cordoba on 8 June but soon
found himself facing a major uprising against the
French. This came to a head at Bailen, 50 miles
east of Cordoba. At the Battle of Bailen (19 July
1808) the French were routed, 17,600 prisoners
were taken and Dupont himself was wounded.
This victory caused a sensation worldwide as it
was the first time that a Napoleonic army had
been beaten.

'The Spanish Bull-Fight' (*above*) – which
also appeared in a Spanish edition – has various
European sovereigns looking down from the
Theatre Royal of Europe as the Spanish bull
tramples on King Joseph and tosses Napoleon.
To the right the wounded bulls crying for help
are Prussia, Holland and Denmark. In 'The Beast'
(*opposite top*) by George Sauley the biblical
monster (note the number 666 on its body) has
heads from all the major countries allied to
France and shows the figure of Spain cutting
off Napoleon's while Hope catches his crown.
And in Gillray's 'Spanish Patriots' (*opposite
bottom*) the French are overwhelmed by the
people of Spain. However, it should be noted that
despite the presence of a solitary British
grenadier and a barrel marked 'British
Gunpowder', no British troops had yet landed
in Spain itself.

The Beast as Described in the Revelations Resembling Napoleon Bonaparte
George Sauley, 22 July 1808

Spanish Patriots Attacking the French Banditti – Loyal Britons Lending a Lift
James Gillray, 15 August 1808

Napoleon the Little in a Rage With His Great French Eagle
Thomas Rowlandson, 20 September 1808

Murat Gives an Account to Napoleon of the Situation in Spain
Spanish print, c.1808

The Spanish continued to harass the French. Meanwhile, after a call for assistance from both the Spanish and Portuguese governments, a British force of 10,000 men under the command of Lieutenant-General Sir Arthur Wellesley landed at Mondego Bay, 110 miles north of Lisbon. Then, aided by Portuguese troops, they headed south towards the capital and defeated the French at the Battle of Obidos (15 August) and the Battle of Roliça (17 August). Next Wellesley, while covering a landing of British reinforcements, beat the French under General Junot at the Battle of Vimeiro (21 August), 32 miles northwest of Lisbon. The French suffered 2000 casualties while Wellesley's force lost only 720. Wellesley was then relieved of command and the Convention of Cintra was signed with the French by which 26,000 French troops and all their baggage were repatriated to France in British ships. Following this Sir John Moore took command of the Allied forces and in November crossed the border into Spain with 30,000 troops, heading for Valladolid.

The Valley of the Shadow of Death
James Gillray, 24 September 1808

What seemed to be the beginning of the end for the French in the Iberian peninsula is shown in these four cartoons. In 'Napoleon in a Rage' (*opposite top*) the Emperor cannot understand the mauling his army has had at the hands of the 'Spanish Cormorants', while the Spanish cartoon (*opposite bottom*) has the Devil handing Napoleon a paper inscribed 'God has more than me' as Commander-in-Chief Marshal Murat (right) makes his report on the disastrous Spanish campaign. In the first of the two cartoons by Gillray (*above*) Napoleon is seen leading a Russian bear between two deadly rivers from Greek mythology – the Lethe and the Styx (in which King Joseph is drowning) – and being faced with the British lion, the Sicilian terrier, the Spanish mule (ridden by Death) and the Portuguese wolf. Two French generals in the clouds say 'Remember Dupont' (at the Battle of Bailen) and 'Remember Junot' (at the Battle of Vimeiro) while an Austrian eagle attacks from behind and various other national creatures express general feelings of ill-will. In the second drawing (*right*) Napoleon appears as a phoenix – the mythical bird that is reborn in flames – being burnt on the peaks of the Pyrenees after his campaign in Spain. (Note that his crown has fallen off, he has a *cordon d'honneur* of daggers around his throat, and a dove of peace arises from the smoke above his head.)

Apotheosis of the Corsican Phoenix
James Gillray, 2 September 1808

Nap and His Partner Joe
Thomas Rowlandson, 29 September 1808

The Flight of Joseph Bonaparte, King of Spain
British print, 1808

**Brobdingnags of Bayonne Peeping over the Pyreneean Mountains
at the Lilliputian Spanish Army**
George Woodward, 31 August 1808

King Joseph entered Madrid in state on 20 July, but without any great welcome from the Spanish people. However, after hearing the news of the major French defeat at Bailen and learning that Spanish forces were now marching on Madrid, he retreated to Vittoria and then across the Pyrenees to Bayonne in southern France a few days later – taking a considerable amount of money and loot with him. Meanwhile, the remaining French troops under the overall command of Marshal Joachim Murat continued to face fierce resistance from the Spanish armies and people.

The drawing by Rowlandson (*opposite top*) has various Spanish commanders kicking Napoleon and Joseph into a dragon's mouth while 'The Flight of Joseph Bonaparte' (*opposite bottom*) has the king (losing his crown) on a mule laden with sacks of gold and treasures racing towards Bayonne pursued by two bulls – John Bull (carrying arms from George III) and its Spanish cousin 'Don Bull' – snorting 'Liberty'. Woodward's 'Brobdingnags of Bayonne' (*above*) is another reference to Jonathan Swift's *Gulliver's Travels* (1726) with the giants Napoleon and Joseph looking down from the Pyrenees on the tiny Spanish defeating the French army, while 'Long Faces' (*right*) has the pair looking very depressed at their current situation.

**Long Faces at Bayonne,
or King Nap and King Joe in the Dumps**
George Woodward, August 1808

1809

THE YEAR 1809 began badly for the British, who now stood alone once more against Napoleonic Europe. At the end of 1808 Sir John Moore's invasion of Spain had failed and he found his route back to Portugal had been cut off. As a result, in January he was forced to march his British expeditionary force of 20,000 men 250 miles through mountainous terrain in winter to the northern port of Corunna. Here they were evacuated – Dunkirk-style – on 100 transports (escorted by 12 ships of the line) though Moore himself was killed in a successful rearguard action at the Battle of Corunna (16 January). The outlook improved briefly in April when Austria joined Britain in the Fifth Coalition and invaded Napoleon's German ally, Bavaria. However, after being defeated at Eckmühl and Regensburg, the Austrians were driven back inside their own borders. They then achieved a major victory at the Battle of Aspern-Essling outside Vienna but were finally beaten at the Battle of Wagram which resulted in the Treaty of Schönbrunn. Britain also began to fight back. After a number of successful naval raids by the maverick Lord Cochrane (including an attack on the French fleet in the Basque Roads in April), Lord Chatham led the so-called Walcheren Expedition which took the island of Walcheren and the seaport of Flushing near The Hague before malaria forced its abandonment. Meanwhile, there were uprisings against French rule in the German states of Westphalia and Brunswick, as well as in the Tyrol. In the Peninsular War the French beat the Spanish at Ocana (giving them all of Andalusia) and took Gerona and Saragossa after long sieges, but were themselves defeated at the battles of Alcaniz and Tamames. Moore's successor, Lieutenant-General Wellesley, also recaptured Oporto and drove the French from Portugal. He then crossed into Spain and defeated them with a joint British and Spanish force at the Battle of Talavera de la Reina near Madrid, a victory which led to him being created Viscount Wellington. On the home front, the deaf, elderly and gout-ridden Duke of Portland retired after 18 months as prime minister to be replaced in October by the lawyer Spencer Perceval.

Pandora Opening Her Box
James Gillray, 22 August 1809

Despite the military activities on the mainland of Europe it seemed that the cartoonists and caricaturists in Britain at this time were mostly concerned with the scandal surrounding the Duke of York, then Commander-in-Chief of the British Army. In January 1809 Colonel Gwylym Lloyd Wardle MP attacked the Duke of York in Parliament, accusing him of making military promotions on the recommendation of his former mistress, the actress Mrs Mary Anne Clarke, who charged the officers concerned a fee for this service. It was also implied that the Duke not only knew of this arrangement but himself shared in the proceeds. A Parliamentary inquiry followed and though MPs voted by a large majority that the Duke was not guilty of corruption, he none the less resigned his position. More than 100 prints were produced concerning this scandal from February to June 1809 alone.

Gillray (*opposite*) has Mrs Clarke facing the inquiry and Rowlandson's drawing (*right*) reprints in picture-riddle form one of the two published letters from the Duke of York to Mrs Clarke. Meanwhile, Cruikshank's 'French Generals Receiving an English Charge' (*below*) shows Napoleon (centre), Talleyrand (left) and a group of French generals looking with amusement at a collection of British caricatures (*portrait-charge* in French). The one which Talleyrand holds is Rowlandson's 'Yorkshire Hieroglyphics!! Plate 1'.

Yorkshire Hieroglyphics!! Plate 1
Thomas Rowlandson, 8 March 1809

French Generals Receiving an English <u>Charge</u>
Isaac Cruikshank, 28 April 1809

The Head of the Family in Good Humour
Thomas Rowlandson, 15 January 1809

A Design for a Monument, to be Erected in Commemoration of the Glorious and Never to be Forgotten Grand Expidition [*sic*] So Ably Planned and Executed in the Year 1809
Thomas Rowlandson, 14 September 1809

Despite the failure of Sir John Moore's expedition in Spain and the sad news of his death, Britain maintained its confidence. However it was still blockaded by Napoleon's Continental System and surrounded by enemies. In an attempt to open up a new front in Europe, General Sir John Pitt, 2nd Earl of Chatham (William Pitt's older brother), led a major expedition of nearly 40,000 troops and more than 260 ships and transports to Walcheren Island on the River Scheldt on the southwest coast of Holland. They landed on 30 July and on 13 August began a bombardment of Flushing (Vlissingen) which included the use of Congreve rockets. Having captured the town on 16 August they then prepared to march on Antwerp to attack its fortress, manned by 35,000 French troops. However, before they could do so, a large proportion of the British

army (more than 11,000 men) succumbed to 'polder fever' (malaria) and typhus and Chatham was forced to evacuate his troops back to England. Of nearly 4000 dead only about 100 were killed in action.

In Rowlandson's first cartoon (*above left*) a giant John Bull looks down at his much smaller opponents (left to right): Napoleon, Russia, Holland, the USA (which had imposed an embargo on trade with Britain in 1807), Prussia, Austria, Spain (now reoccupied by the French) and Denmark.

In the second cartoon (*above right*) the 1st Earl of Chatham (William Pitt the Elder) is shown grieving at his son's failure in the Walcheren Expedition, while John Bull (left) and Jack Tar stand dejected. Meanwhile, Dutch frogs smoke their pipes and French monkeys are seen 'in attitudes of derision'.

The Siege of Vienna
French print, 1809

After defeating the Austrians in quick succession at Abensberg, Landeshut, Eckmühl and Regensburg, Napoleon next laid siege to Vienna which capitulated on 13 May 1809. However, the Austrian army under Archduke Charles then regrouped and faced Napoleon's troops five miles east of the city near the villages of Aspern and Essling on the north bank of the River Danube. The Battle of Aspern-Essling (21-22 May 1809) was fought fiercely but after a number of reverses the Austrians won and the French retreated. This was first major defeat of Napoleon himself. Austrian losses were 23,000 while the French lost more than 21,000 including the death of Napoleon's friend, Marshal Jean Lannes – one of the first to be created marshal (and the first one to die).

A Sacrifice to Ambition
John Boyne, 12 December 1803

After the Battle of Aspern-Essling Napoleon retreated to the nearby island of Lobau (situated in the middle of the River Danube four miles east of Vienna) and turned it into a fortified base. From here he advanced to the village of Wagram, 11 miles northeast of the capital, where he was met by Archduke Charles's forces. The Battle of Wagram (5-6 July) ended with a victory for Napoleon but heavy losses – about 23,000 were killed or wounded and 7000 missing (Austrian losses were 19,000 plus about 6700 missing). Austria signed the Treaty of Schönbrunn on 14 October.

In the first of these two critical cartoons on French and British ambition (*left*) the British artist John Boyne (1750-1810) shows Napoleon in classical armour standing in front of an altar covered in skulls and military trophies as a Fury gives him a chalice of blood. Below him a dragon can be seen roaring in the nearby abyss, behind him stands the figure of Death and in the clouds above Justice awaits with her scales. The French print (*below*), by contrast, has George III as a tiger being attacked by a harpy for funding the war against Napoleon. In the background Prussia nurses a bloody nose while Mercury offers more gold to Tsar Alexander I of Russia.

Ambition Dominates Him
French print, November 1806

Andreas Hofer and His Adjutants
German print, 1809

One of the many national revolts against French rule was in the mountainous area of southern Austria known as the Tyrol, which had been transferred from Austrian to (pro-French) Bavarian rule after the Treaty of Pressburg (1805). In April 1809 a successful rebellion was led by an innkeeper from St Leonhard called Andreas Hofer. However, following Austria's defeat later in the year, Bavarian rule was confirmed by the Treaty of Schönbrunn. Hofer himself then fled into the mountains but was caught in January 1810, taken to Mantua and executed. In this German print (*above*), Hofer is the central figure.

On the Iberian Peninsula, following the evacuation of Sir John Moore's troops from Corunna, the British forces regrouped in Portugal under Sir Arthur Wellesley and after driving the French from Oporto (12 May) and out of Portugal began another invasion of Spain in July 1809. Marching northeast from Lisbon along the valley of the River Tagus with a joint British and Spanish army, Wellesley crossed the border into Spain and reached Talavera de la Reina, 70 miles southwest of Madrid. Here he halted to consolidate his supplies but was attacked at night by a French army under Marshal Claude Victor. The Battle of Talavera (27-28 July 1809) resulted in a victory for the Allies with the British suffering 800 killed, nearly 4000 wounded and 650 missing and the Spanish claiming a loss of 1200 killed or wounded (French losses were 760 killed, 6400 wounded and 200 missing). Though Wellesley then withdrew back into Portugal in the face of a large French force under Marshal Soult, he was created Viscount Wellington as a result of this victory.

A Wellington Boot, or the Head of the Army
Paul Pry (William Heath), 1827

The successes of the Duke of Wellington have been commemorated in a number of ways, mostly famously in the Wellington boot, shown here (*right*) in a later drawing by William Heath (1795-1840). Originally a high leather boot covering the knees in front and cut away behind, the word nowadays refers to a waterproof rubber boot reaching to the knee. Also named after him are Wellington College, the giant fir tree *Wellingtonia*, and the dish Beef Wellington.

1810-11

HAVING CAPTURED Martinique in 1809, the British took Guadeloupe, France's last possession in the Caribbean, in February 1810, and later in the year also the French islands of Mauritius and Reunion in the Indian Ocean. In the Peninsular War – by now described by Napoleon as 'The Spanish Ulcer' – the French eventually took the fortified border town of Ciudad Rodrigo and invaded Portugal. Wellington then withdrew to Lisbon, around which he had built a three-line defencework known as the Lines of Torres Vedras. This year also saw the beginning of the long siege of Cadiz, a major seaport and naval base and capital of free Spain which had a large (25,000) British and Portuguese garrison supplied by the Royal Navy.

In 1811, apart from the British conquest of the fortified island of Java in the Dutch East Indies (now Indonesia), the main focus of the war was again the Iberian Peninsula. It began with the first two of three sieges of the strongly fortified town of Badajos on the Spanish-Portuguese border. The first assault (January-May) was a success for the French against the Spanish. The second siege (May-June), led by the British under General Beresford against the French, failed and Beresford abandoned it to fight a major battle to halt the French advance at nearby La Albuera. Eventually won by the Allies, it was a fiercely fought and bloody battle. Meanwhile, the British defeated the French at Fuentes De Onoro on the Spanish border near Ciudad Rodrigo, and the Battle of Coimbra near Lisbon proved a turning point, forcing the French to leave Portugal altogether in April. There was also great rejoicing in Britain at news of the capture of the first French eagle at the Battle of Barrossa near Cadiz.

On the domestic front, this year the increasing illness of George III led to the establishment of the Regency under his eldest son, the Prince of Wales (the future George IV). Also, having divorced his wife Josephine in 1809, Napoleon married Archduchess Marie-Louise of Austria, daughter of Emperor Francis I, the following year. In 1811 she gave birth to their son, the King of Rome.

The Archduchess Maria Louisa Going to Take Her Nap
British print, 12 April 1810

On 2 April 1810 Napoleon married the Archduchess Marie-Louise of Austria, daughter of Emperor Francis I (ironically, her great-aunt was Louis XVI's wife Marie-Antoinette, who had been executed by the French Revolutionary leaders shortly after her husband).

Napoleon had married the 18-year-old Marie-Louise because he wanted an heir. However, the British cartoon (*left*) expresses the new bride's disappointment on their wedding night.

British Cookery or 'Out of the Frying Pan into the Fire'
British print, *The Scourge*, May 1811

The first siege of the fortress of Ciudad Rodrigo on the Agueda River, 53 miles southwest of Salamanca, took place between 30 May and 9 June 1810. Defended by 6500 Spanish troops under Don Andres Herrarti it was finally taken after bombardment by the French under Marshal Michel Ney. French losses were 180 killed and 1000 wounded while the Spanish lost 60 killed, nearly 1000 wounded and 4000 taken prisoner. This left the route to Lisbon open to the French who invaded Portugal soon afterwards. Wellington (as he now was) then retreated towards the capital, beating the French on the way at the Battle of Bussaco (27 September), 120 miles northeast of Lisbon. Once behind the Lines of Torres Vedras, the Allies were besieged by Marshal André Masséna who arrived with 60,000 men on 11 October but was eventually forced to retreat.

The following year, in the first siege of Badajos (26 January -9 March 1811), a strongly fortified Spanish town four miles from the Portuguese border, the Spanish surrendered to the French under Marshal Soult. Once in French hands it was then besieged by Allied forces under British Lieutenant-General Sir William Carr Beresford (who in 1806 had captured Buenos Aires). During this second siege (6 May-12 June 1811) Marshal Soult led a relief force which fought

the Allies at the Battle of La Albuera (16 May 1811). Called the 'most murderous and sanguinary' conflict of the entire Peninsular War, it took place near the village of La Albuera, 13 miles southeast of Badajoz. British (including Hanoverian), Spanish and Portuguese troops, under the command of Beresford, eventually prevailed but at great cost. The British lost more than half their men (3900 killed or wounded out of 7600) and the total Allied loss was 6000. French losses were 7000. During the battle, Lieutenant-Colonel William Inglis was badly wounded and called out to his regiment: 'Die hard, 57th! Die hard!' They did, and the 57th (later the Middlesex Regiment) were subsequently known as 'the Die Hards'.

In 'British Cookery' (*above*) from the satirical magazine *The Scourge*, Wellington (left) has in his left hand a large frying pan (labelled 'Portugal') containing French soldiers while with his right hand he bastes the French eagle (with the head of Masséna) with a 'British Basting Ladle'. To his left are (above) Napoleon in a stewpot and (below) Junot in a pickle jar, while at the right General Thomas Graham (victor of the Battle of Barrosa, 5 March 1811) uses the bellows of 'British Bravery' to raise the flames.

With the increasing madness of George III (which was later diagnosed as being due to the hereditary disease porphyria) the Prince of Wales was finally sworn in as Regent on 6 February 1811. Not well liked by the public, the middle-aged and overweight 'Prinny' had a reputation as a womaniser. He was also very proud of his appointment as Colonel-Commandant of the Tenth Light Dragoons and personally designed a new uniform for himself and his men which he wore as often as possible.

Gillray's drawing (*right*) of a proposed statue to the Prince of Wales celebrates this appointment and shows him mounted on his favourite horse, Pegasus. Cruikshank's later cartoon (*below*) comments on his increasing obesity and portrays him as a huge whale swimming in the Sea of Politics. He is spouting 'The Liquor of Oblivion' (left) over outgoing Whig politicians Grey (as a dog), Grenville (as a turtle) and Sheridan, and 'The Dew of Favour' (right) over new Prime Minister Spencer Perceval and his followers in a boat, while the Prince's mistress Lady Hertford (as a mermaid) looks on.

Hint to Modern Sculptors, as an Ornament to a Future Square
James Gillray, 3 May 1796

Prince of Whales, or the Fisherman at Anchor
George Cruikshank, *The Scourge*, 1812

George III's third son, the Duke of Clarence (later William IV), who had had an active naval career before war broke out, became Admiral of the Fleet in 1811. Meanwhile, the same year, George's second son, Frederick the Duke of York, returned to office as Commander-in-Chief of the army having been forced to resign in 1809 over the cash-for-military-honours scandal involving his former mistress, Mrs Clarke (see p.91).

In 'A True British Tar' (*right*) Gillray draws the Duke of Clarence as a common sailor and puns on 'jordan' (the name for a chamber pot) which was also the surname of the duke's mistress, the actress Dora Jordan. Meanwhile, in 'The Return to Office', from the monthly magazine *The Scourge*, Prime Minister Spencer Perceval is seen sweeping away the Duke of York's accusers as the Prince of Wales – now Prince Regent – invites him back to the War Office headquarters at Horse Guards in London.

A True British Tar
James Gillray, 28 May 1795

The Return to Office
George Cruikshank, *The Scourge*, 1811

**Nursing the Spawn of a Tyrant,
or Frenchmen Sick of the Breed**
Thomas Rowlandson, 14 April 1811

At 9.20am on 20 March 1811 the Empress Marie-Louise gave birth to a son, Napoleon King of Rome. In Rowlandson's cartoon (*left*) Napoleon watches from behind a curtain as Marie-Louise fends off the infant on her lap who is trying to stab her with one hand while holding the imperial orb in the other. As she does so she claims the child's grandfather must be the devil himself. Talleyrand (left), wearing a mitre, holds out a cup labelled 'Composing Draught' and advises her to send him to his grandfather as soon as possible. The French print (*below*), by contrast, is more flattering (note the French eagle in the foreground).

French print, 1811

**Devils Among the Flats, or Boney Getting Into Hot Water –
the First Glorious Exploit of the Invincible Boulogne Flotilla, 20 September 1811**
British print, September 1811

A comet appeared in the sky above Europe in 1811-12 which led to many allusions in cartoons of this time. In this anonymous drawing (*above*) it is the late Admiral Nelson whose head forms the comet (lightning bolts from the tail of which – inscribed 'Remember Nelson' – are directed at Napoleon). The scene below is based on a real incident which took place at Boulogne during a visit by Napoleon. Twenty-seven French vessels – some of them as large as frigates – were attacked and badly damaged in the coastal shallows (mudflats) by a British force of five (the *Naiad*, three sloops and a cutter). Napoleon (seen here with Marshal Ney in the left-hand boat labelled 'Napoleon le Grand') berates the captain and steersman of one of the ships – which has returned from the battle much damaged and full of corpses – and threatens to sink the boat himself.

1812

FOR MANY the famous Great Comet that first appeared in the sky in March 1811, and could be seen in Russia until August 1812, was taken as an omen and this year saw a massive change in the fortunes of Napoleon. In the Peninsular War Wellington began by taking the Spanish border fortress of Ciudad Rodrigo back from the French in January. He then swung south to attack the other gateway into Spain at Badajos in April. Ultimately successful, but at great cost (this infamous third siege of the city has been described as the greatest slaughter in the smallest space of any battle in the nineteenth century), he marched into northern Spain. Here he won his most important victory in Europe to date at Salamanca in July, entered Madrid in August, but unable to take Burgos in October, retired back to winter quarters in Portugal.

Meanwhile, Napoleon's invasion of Russia in June – without a formal declaration of war – led to the formation of the Sixth Coalition (Britain, Portugal, Spain and Russia) against France. After crossing the Russian border at Kovno (now Lithuania) on the River Niemen his enormous Grand Army – by now numbering some 675,000 troops from many countries – passed through Vilna (Vilnius) and defeated the Russians at Mogilev near Minsk (now capital of Belarus) before crossing the River Dnieper. The Grand Army then drove though the Russian plains until Tsar Alexander I finally made a stand in September at the Battle of Borodino outside Moscow, Russia's ancient religious centre (the capital was then at St Petersburg). After a bloody but indecisive battle the Russians withdrew. Napoleon then marched into Moscow to find that the Russian army had abandoned it, and the following day the city burst into flames. Receiving no surrender terms from the Tsar, the early onset of winter eventually forced the French to retreat. Harried by guerrillas and lacking supplies, the Grand Army eventually crossed the River Beresina near Minsk in freezing weather. Shortly afterwards Napoleon abandoned his troops and returned to Paris. By the time the remains of his army recrossed the Niemen to safety on 14 December, it had been all but destroyed, having lost 570,000 men and 200,000 horses.

On 11 May 1812 Spencer Perceval was shot and killed in the Lobby of the House of Commons in London – the first (and to date only) British prime minister to be assassinated. He was replaced by Lord Liverpool (formerly Lord Hawkesbury), who remained in office for almost 15 years (until February 1827), making him the longest-serving British prime minister ever.

The Prime Crutch – Lord Liverpool
George Cruikshank, c.1819.

At the beginning of 1812 Wellington began a new Spanish campaign and, leaving Portugal, began to besiege the border fortress of Ciudad Rodrigo, on 8 January. The British took the fort on the 19th. Wellington then turned south to attack the fortified border town of Badajoz in one of the bloodiest sieges of the nineteenth century. Beginning on 16 March 1812 the town was eventually taken on 6 April. The victorious Allied soldiers then embarked on a three-day drunken spree in which many outrages were committed against the defenceless population. Having cleared the gates to Spain Wellington next invaded the north of the country and on 17 June attacked the French at Salamanca, 107 miles west northwest of Madrid. In a brilliant victory – his greatest in Europe up to this time – Wellington destroyed the army of Marshal Auguste de Marmont. The French lost 14,000 including 7000 taken prisoner, while Allied losses were only around 5000. Soon afterwards Wellington headed south. He entered Madrid on 12 August and on the 24th raised the two-year siege of Cadiz, the major naval base (and capital of free Spain) near Gibraltar, which had begun on 5 February 1810.

The two cartoons reproduced here show the huge French mortar mounted on a cast-iron Chinese dragon which had been used to besiege Cadiz but had been abandoned by the French after Wellington's victory at Salamanca and the subsequent raising of the siege. The mortar – the largest of its day – was presented to the Prince Regent by the Spanish people and was originally installed in Horse Guards Parade, London. The inscription reads: 'To commemorate the raising of the siege of Cadiz in consequence of the glorious victory gained by the Duke of Wellington over the French near Salamanca, 22 July 1812.' As a mortar was then called a 'bomb' (pronounced 'bum'), the Cadiz memorial was also known as the 'Regent's Bomb' and hence the punning cartoon by Williams (*top*) showing a rear view of the Prince Regent. The mortar also appears in many later prints, including jokes involving his mistress Lady Hertford and one (*right*) in which the Prince Regent is shown trying to get his own back on the satirists.

A View of the R-g-t's Bomb
Charles Williams, August 1816

**His Most Gracious Majesty Hum IVth
and His Ministers Going to Play the Devil With the Satirists**
British print, 1820

The Bear, the Bull Dog and the Monkey
William Heath, 24 August 1812

Ignoring Wellington's successes in Spain, Napoleon now embarked on a war on two fronts. On 24 June the Grand Army crossed the River Niemen that marked the Russian border.

After pausing for a few weeks at Vilna (Vilnius) and Vitebsk the French rapidly marched towards the ancient city of Moscow, fighting a number of battles on the way, including the bloody but indecisive Battle of Smolensk (17 August). The Russians continued to retreat – burning towns and crops in their wake to deny supplies to the French – and finally made a stand at Borodino, a village 70 miles west southwest of Moscow. The Battle of Borodino (5-7 September 1812) – also known as the Battle of Moscow – resulted in a French victory but at huge cost. Napoleon lost 33,000 troops while his opponent, 67-year-old General Mikhail Kutuzov, had 44,000 casualties including the distinguished general Prince Petr Bagration who was mortally wounded. After Borodino the Russians withdrew and left Moscow undefended. On 14 September Napoleon marched into the city, but two days later it was engulfed in flames.

Ivan Terebenev, Russian print, c.1812

The Burning of Moscow
George Cruikshank in William Combe, *The Life of Napoleon* (1815)

In Heath's drawing (*opposite top*) the Russian bear grabs the monkey Napoleon and bites his hat while the British bulldog (note the collar inscribed 'Wellington') goes for his throat. The scroll on the ground reads: 'French policy. Fraud, Cruelty and Treachery'. Meanwhile (*opposite below*), the Russian artist Ivan Terebenev (1780-1815) mocks the lack of prisoners taken by the French by showing them pulling along a trolley containing dummies dressed as Cossacks. Cruikshank (*above*) depicts Napoleon's anguish as he looks out on the burning buildings of historic Moscow while the Russian cartoon (*right*) has him approaching hell along a road covered in skeletons as his sceptre and imperial crown fall to the ground. In the clouds God's all-seeing eye appears with one hand pointing to a rebuilt Moscow and another holding a flaming scourge above Napoleon's head.

Napoleon After the Burning of Moscow
Russian print, 1812

General Frost Shaving Little Boney
William Elmes, 1 December 1812

Napoleon had intended to spend the winter of 1812 in Moscow and then march on the capital, St Petersburg. However, five weeks later – faced with Moscow in flames, no official delegation offering to surrender the city, and the onset of snow and frost (heralding the earliest Russian winter in 40 years) – he had no option but to retreat back to France the way he had come. His problems were made worse by the fact that the scorched-earth policy of the Russians had left nothing for the French to supplement their already overstretched supply line, and the Grand Army was soon reduced to tatters as it retraced its steps.

These cartoons show the desperate situation of the French. In the drawing (*left*) by William Elmes (fl.1811-20), General Frost is a frightening hybrid of the Russian bear and an ice monster which crushes French soldiers beneath its feet and shaves Napoleon with 'Russian Steel' while Riga, St Petersburg and Moscow can be seen in flames in the background. The Russian cartoon (*below*) has Boor Babeela Moroz – the Russian equivalent of Jack Frost – chasing after Napoleon and his marshals in the form of hares. Meanwhile, Cruikshank's drawing (*opposite top*) comments on the regular bulletins that Napoleon sent back to France while on campaign. In the bulletin he sent from Russia to Paris on 27 October 1812 he said: 'it is beautiful weather ... this weather will last eight days longer' (in fact snow began to fall on 13 October).

The Russian Boor Babeela Moroz Hunting Hares
Russian print, 1812

Boney Hatching a Bulletin, or Snug Winter Quarters!!!
George Cruikshank, 1812

Review of the French Troops on Their Returning March Through Smolensko
George Cruikshank, 27 May 1813

On its retreat from Moscow the Grand Army fought a successful defensive action 60 miles southwest of the city at the Battle of Maloyaroslavets (24 October) – during which Napoleon himself was nearly captured by Cossacks. On 9 November it arrived back in the gruesome former battlefield of Smolensk – still littered with bodies – and soon after fought off another major Russian attack near St Petersburg at the Battle of Krasnoi (17 November). It then entered Byelorussia (Belarus) en route to Poland and Paris, harried all the way by Russian partisans.

The Cruikshank drawing (*above*), published long after the events it depicts, has been redrawn after a Russian original.

The Pig Messenger
Russian print, 1812

Journey of the Exalted Traveller from Warsaw to Paris
Ivan Terebenev, 1812

The Corsican Bloodhound Beset by the Bears of Russia
William Elmes, 7 March 1813

By 22 November when the French reached the River Beresina – a tributary of the Dnieper 45 miles northeast of the Byelorussian capital of Minsk – the Grand Army had been reduced to only 49,000 effective troops. Here they discovered that the bridge at Borisov – the only crossing to the safety of Vilna in French-ruled Poland – had been destroyed by the Russians. In consequence Napoleon ordered the construction of a pontoon bridge nine miles north of Borisov and began to cross there. The Russians soon discovered their movements but after a fierce rearguard battle the bulk of the French army managed to cross in appalling conditions. Napoleon then ordered the bridge to be burnt and thousands of camp followers died or were drowned in the panic not to be left behind. The French lost 25,000 men during the battle (as well as 30,000 non-combatants) and the Russians killed a further 10,000 stragglers. After crossing the Beresina Napoleon led his army back through Poland, but deserted his troops at Smorgonia on 4 December and headed back to Paris in disguise. Meanwhile, the remains of the Grand Army crossed the Niemen once more near Kovno and then marched south to Warsaw. Of the 600,000 troops who had crossed the Niemen for the conquest of Russia only 20,000 marched back over the bridge at Kovno. News of the destruction of the Grand Army was published in London on 16 December (*The Times* called it 'a divine judgement').

These three cartoons sum up Napoleon's plight. 'The Pig Messenger' (*top*) shows Napoleon crossing the skeleton-strewn River Niemen near Kovno (seen in the background) and carrying an upside-down figure of Glory (with its feathers falling out) on his back. As he orders an armed pig to take a despatch to Paris announcing his return a Russian soldier can be seen in the clouds wielding a knout. The drawing by Terebenev (*centre*) has Napoleon with a French general on his shoulders driving a sledge furiously towards Paris and dragging a tattered French eagle and wounded Mameluke guard. Meanwhile, the drawing by Elmes (*bottom*) has Napoleon trying to escape while dragging the 'Moscow Kettle' out of which fall papers which read 'Death', 'Famine', 'Destruction' etc.

In the first of these two cartoons Elmes (*right*) draws a sequel to Gillray's earlier 'Valley of the Shadow of Death' cartoon (see p.87). This time Napoleon confronts not the British lion but the Russian bear with the figure of Death on its back. Amongst the many other figures shown the main ones are (anticlockwise from right) the British lion and bulldog, General Frost (blowing a 'Russian Scourge' at Napoleon) and the Muscovy cat. Cruikshank's 'Murat Reviewing the Grand Army' (*below*) has a freezing Marshal Murat, mounted on a skinny horse labelled 'Boney Part', gazing in horror at the decrepit troops of which he has just been given command.

The Valley of the Shadow of Death
William Elmes, December 1812

Murat Reviewing the Grand Army!!!!!!
George Cruikshank, January 1813

1813

AFTER THE RETREAT from Moscow the writing was on the wall for Napoleon. In February Prussia joined the Sixth Coalition against France (followed in May by Austria and Sweden), and began the German War of Liberation. However, the Allies were at first defeated in a number of battles in pro-French Saxony – at Lützen, Bautzen, and at the Saxon capital of Dresden, in what was to prove Napoleon's last major victory on German soil. While retreating from Dresden the Allies defeated the French at Kulm to the south of the city. Napoleon then marched on Berlin but was checked on the outskirts of the Prussian capital at the battles of Grossbeeren and Dennewitz in September. Having twice failed to take Berlin Napoleon fell back to the Saxon city of Leipzig where he received a major blow. The Battle of Leipzig in October – also known as the Battle of the Nations – was not only the largest battle of the Napoleonic Wars but also the largest battle in European history up until that time. The result was a victory for the Allies but at a huge cost, nearly 50,000 being killed or wounded on each side.

Meanwhile, things were also going badly for Napoleon in the Peninsular War. Taking advantage of the withdrawal of French troops from the area following Napoleon's setbacks in Russia and Central Europe, Wellington led a British, Portuguese and Spanish invasion force out of Portugal and claimed a major victory in June at the Battle of Vittoria near Pamplona, which led King Joseph to flee across the Pyrenees into France. Wellington then captured the garrison at Pamplona, the last major French stronghold on Spanish soil, pursued Napoleon's forces across the border and defeated them at the Battle of the Nivelle in November, the first to be fought in France itself.

The Hero's Return
George Cruikshank, 22 February 1813

Having deserted his troops on 4 December, Napoleon arrived in Paris on the 18th. The Grand Army itself eventually reached the French capital, in a dismal state, and was put under the command of Marshal Murat. Undeterred, Napoleon quickly began to rebuild his forces using 15- and 16-year-old boys known as 'Les Marie-Louises' (so-called after his wife who, as regent in his absence, had signed the conscription order) and on 10 January the French Senate promised 350,000 new recruits.

'The Hero's Return' (*opposite*) mocks the flattering paintings of Napoleon by the French Revolutionary artist Jacques-Louis David (Cruikshank has jokingly signed it 'David *pinxit*'). However, in this version Napoleon is seen arriving back at the Tuileries Palace carried by a Mameluke guard (and supported by two others) and minus his nose, an ear and the fingers of both hands as a result of frostbite (all seen preserved in various bottles). He is greeted by a shocked Empress Marie-Louise as well as Napoleon's three sisters and his screaming son, the King of Rome. 'A Medical Consultation' by Ivan Terebenev (*above right*) has one doctor feeling Napoleon's pulse while another examines his tongue. Their verdict is that he is hot-headed and has little pulse left after too much bloodletting. 'French Conscripts' (*right*) comments on 'Les Marie-Louises' and has Napoleon (note the initials 'NB' on his sword belt) – minus an eye, his nose and both legs – urging children to join his new Grand Army.

A Medical Consultation
Ivan Terebenev, 1812

French Conscripts for the Years 1820, 21, 22, 23, 24 and 25
Marching to Join the Grand Army
George Cruikshank, 18 March 1813

John Bull's Patent Medicine
British print, 28 August 1813

In order to rebuild his Grand Army after the disastrous Russian campaign, Napoleon began to withdraw troops from the Iberian Peninsula. Seeing his chance, Wellington once more invaded northern Spain from Portugal, and beat the French under Marshal Jourdan and Joseph Bonaparte, King of Spain, at a decisive victory at Vittoria, 50 miles west of Pamplona. At the Battle of Vittoria (21 June 1813) Jourdan also lost his marshal's baton which was sent to the Prince Regent in London, who in turn sent Wellington a field marshal's baton of his own. Though the victory would have been even more complete had the Allied soldiers not celebrated by looting and drinking (it was after this battle that Wellington referred to his troops as 'the scum of the earth'), the Battle of Vittoria effectively ended French rule in

Spain and King Joseph fled across the Pyrenees to France. The victory was greeted with great celebrations in London and elsewhere. On 7 October Wellington crossed the border and entered France itself, defeating Marshal Soult's forces on the River Nivelle at the Battle of the Nivelle (10 November).

In 'John Bull's Patent Medicine' (*above*) Napoleon (right) is shown being purged of his crowns by 'Wellington's Mixture' as doctor John Bull looks on. The title of the cartoon by Williams (*opposite top*) alludes to '*Veni, vidi, vici*' ('I came, I saw, I conquered'), the words allegedly used by Julius Caesar after his victory at Zela in 47BC. Meanwhile, Cruikshank (*opposite bottom*) depicts the Vauxhall Fete held in London's Vauxhall Gardens in honour of the victory at Vittoria.

Wellington and Glory, or the Victory of Vittoria – He Came, He Saw, He Conquered
Charles Williams, 1813

George Cruikshank, c.1813

Cool Summer Quarters, or Going on <u>Swimmingly</u>!!!!
George Cruikshank, 2 October 1813

On 11 August 1813, less than a month after the Battle of Vittoria, Austria joined the Sixth Coalition and declared war on France. The German War of Liberation had begun in February but the Allies had been defeated at first in a number of battles in pro-French Saxony. In the Battle of Lützen (2 May 1813), a joint Prussian and Russian army lost 20,000 (French losses were 18,000) and the Prussian Commander-in-Chief, General Blücher, was wounded. At the indecisive Battle of Bautzen (20-21 May), 32 miles northeast of Dresden, the Allies lost 13,500 while French casualties were 20,000, including Napoleon's close friend General Geraud Duroc, who was mortally wounded. Then at the Saxon capital of Dresden,

Napoleon won his last major victory on German soil. At the Battle of Dresden (26-27 August) the Allies – who by now also included Austria – lost 16,000 with 15,000 taken prisoner, while the French lost 10,000. Amongst the Allied casualties was the French-born General Victor Moreau who was mortally wounded. While retreating from Dresden the Allies defeated the French at Kulm to the south of the city. Napoleon now marched on Berlin but was checked on the outskirts of the Prussian capital at the battles of Grossbeeren (23 August) and Dennewitz (6 September). In the latter battle the Allies were joined by a large army led by the former French Marshal Bernadotte, now Crown Prince of Sweden.

Cruikshank's 'Cool Summer Quarters' (*opposite*) refers back to his drawing about Napoleon's 'Snug Winter Quarters' on the retreat from Moscow (see p.107) and has Allied soldiers prodding Napoleon and his army literally into 'hot water' at the point of their bayonets. The two drawings by the German artist Gottfried Schadow (1764-1850) depict the situation outside Berlin. In 'Seize Berlin' (*top*), Napoleon can be seen standing on a hill and giving orders while protected by his Mameluke bodyguard. The Grand Army marches behind while at the front left 'Madame Administration' accompanies the non-combatants. 'The Halle Gate' (*below*) has Prussian and Russian (note the armed bear) troops defending one of the ancient gates to Berlin against the effete French invaders.

Seize Berlin!
Gottfried Schadow, December 1813

The Halle Gate – 22 August 1813
Gottfried Schadow, December 1813

Loiterers in the Rue du Coq in Paris
British version of French print, 1814

Very Slippy Weather
James Gillray, 10 February 1808

Caricature Curiosity – Plate 2
George Woodward, 1806

The Caricature Vendor
Dutch print, 1814

Good Humour
British print, 1829

Printshops were a great source of attraction at this time and crowds would gather outside to see the latest caricatures displayed in their windows. In London the best known publishers of Napoleonic War prints included Hannah Humphrey in St James's Street, Samuel Fores (who called himself 'Caricaturist to the First Consul') on the corner of Piccadilly and Sackville Street, Rudolph Ackermann in the Strand, Thomas Tegg in Cheapside, and William Holland in Cockspur Street (near what would soon be christened Trafalgar Square). One of the best known French printshops was Martinet in Rue du Coq, Paris. Prints were also sold on the street by caricature vendors.

'Loiterers in the Rue du Coq' (*opposite top*) shows a crowd outside Martinet's shop at 13-15 Rue du Coq, which ran between the Place de L'Oratoire and the Rue St Honoré, near the Palais Royal. This version of a French original was produced by Thomas Tegg in London and includes an advertisement (left) for Tegg's own shop. (It has also spelt the owner's

name wrong and printed the wrong street number.) Gillray's drawing (*opposite bottom left*) depicts an accident outside Hannah Humphrey's shop at 27 St James's Street, which was also Gillray's home and studio. Note the Guardsman looking at the caricatures in the window, the second row of which displays two Napoleonic War cartoons, 'Tiddy Doll the Great French Gingerbread Maker' (see p.74) and 'The King of Brobdingnag and Gulliver' (see p.55). Woodward's drawing (*opposite bottom right*) has 'Parson Puzzle Text' and a volunteer captain looking at prints of themselves in the window of Holland's shop. The Dutch print (*above left*) shows Napoleon himself as a wayside caricature vendor selling 17 prints of himself by W. Esser, including 'The Cossack's Spear' (see p.118) and 'Napoleon Riding a Cock to Elba' (see p.135). 'Good Humour' (*above right*) has the Duke of Wellington examining a print about himself by William Heath in McLean's window.

The Two Kings of Terror
Thomas Rowlandson, November 1813

The Cossack's Spear
W.Esser, 1813

The Cossack Extinguisher
William Elmes, 10 November 1813

The Parisian Nutcracker
German print, 1813

Having twice failed to take Berlin, Napoleon now fell back to the Saxon city of Leipzig, 10 miles southwest of the Prussian capital, where he received a major blow. The Battle of Leipzig (16-19 October) – also known as the Battle of the Nations because so many countries were involved – was not only the largest battle of the Napoleonic Wars but also the largest battle in European history up until that time. The Allied forces from Austria, Prussia, Russia and Sweden – plus a British Congreve rocket battery – numbered nearly 350,000 against Napoleon's 200,000. During the course of the battle the Bavarians changed sides to join the Allies. The Allies won but at a huge cost, nearly 55,000 being killed or wounded (French losses were 38,000 killed or wounded and 30,000 taken prisoner).

In Rowlandson's cartoon (*opposite top*) the two Kings of Terror are Napoleon (seated on a drum) and Death (sitting on a cannon) – at their feet is a French eagle broken in two. To the left can be seen Allied troops under the flags of (left to right) Russia, Prussia, Austria and Sweden as the French run off in confusion to the right. 'The Cossack Extinguisher' (*opposite bottom right*) has a huge Russian Cossack placing his fur hat – shaped like a conical candle-extinguisher – over a tiny Napoleon. In the background is the walled city of Leipzig. The Dutch cartoon (*opposite bottom left*) by Esser has a Cossack horseman spearing Napoleon with the same message. Meanwhile, the anonymous German cartoon (*above*) has Napoleon trying unsuccessfully to crack a walnut marked 'Leipzig' in his teeth (note that four teeth have already come out in the process and have fallen onto the base of skulls and human bones).

**Dutch Nightmare, or the Fraternal Hug returned
with a Dutch Squeeze**
Thomas Rowlandson, 29 November 1813

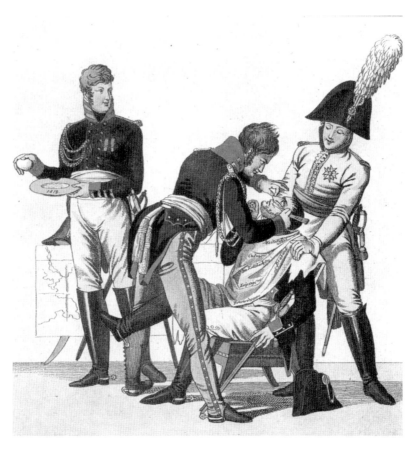

The New European Barbershop
Johann Michael Voltz, 1813

Work Rewarded
W.Esser, 1 January 1814

Napoleon's defeat at the Battle of Leipzig encouraged the other occupied countries of Europe to follow Germany's lead and throw off the yoke of French domination. The Dutch were the first to revolt and the Prince of Orange returned to Holland from exile in Britain in November. There was great support for the Dutch in Britain with many people wearing orange, and 'Orange Boven' ('Up with Orange') became a popular catchphrase. The French evacuated Amsterdam on 16 November and the liberation of the whole of Holland took place shortly afterwards.

Rowlandson's 'Dutch Nightmare' (*above left*) alludes to the famous painting by Henry Fuseli. In this version it is Napoleon in the bed (note the fleur-de-lys pattern on the bedding and two imperial fasces by his feet) and a pipe-smoking Dutchman sits on his chest. The German cartoon (*above right*) by Johann Michael Voltz (1784-1858) has King Frederick William III of Prussia shaving off 'Holland' from Napoleon's beard, as Emperor Francis I of Austria holds him down and Tsar Alexander I of Russia (holding the soap) looks on. The Dutch cartoon (*opposite*) by Esser has Napoleon, kneeling over a drum, being beaten by Dutch soldiers.

Sharing Out the World
Gottfried Schadow, 1813

The Universal Monarch
German print, 1813

'Commencement du Finale'
Gottfried Schadow, 1813

At the end of 1813 Napoleon's position was perilous in the extreme. 'Sharing Out the World' (*opposite top*) by the German artist Gottfried Schadow mocks the pretensions of Napoleon trying to share the world between his marshals (Jerome Bonaparte appears on Napoleon's right) as he is no longer in a position to do this. 'The Universal Monarch' (*opposite bottom*), though published in London, is from a German original (it was also published in Holland) and shows Napoleon sitting on a pile of skulls, including that of the Duc d'Enghien, with his feet on the Treaties of Tilsit and Lunéville and the Peace of Moscow burning on the top of the pile next to him. Napoleon's loyal supporter Grand Marshal Bertrand offers a cup of tears while the eagles of Prussia, Austria and Russia fling

thunderbolts at him. The second cartoon by Schadow (*above*) – whose French title alludes to the words alleged to have been said by Talleyrand after the Battle of Leipzig – has Napoleon (centre) listening to a performance of the 'Leipzig Concerto'. The performers are (left to right): Emperor Francis I of Austria (violin), Prince Charles-Jean (the former French Marshal Bernadotte who later became King Charles XIV) of Sweden (flute) and King Frederick William III of Prussia (cello). The conductor (seated left on a barrel of gunpowder, and holding a cannon as a baton) is Tsar Alexander I of Russia. In the puppet theatre behind them can be seen all the fast-disappearing kings and princelings of the Confederacy of the Rhine created by Napoleon.

WITH THE FALL of Lerida in January 1814, the French were finally driven from Spain and Wellington's forces pushed ever deeper into the heart of France itself, winning victories at Orthez in February (at which Wellington was wounded) and Tarbes in March. Meanwhile, the Russians and Prussians crossed the French border at the River Rhine, the Austrians under Field Marshal Schwartzenberg attacked from Switzerland and the Swedish under Napoleon's former marshal Bernadotte (now Crown Prince Charles-Jean) invaded from Belgium. However, Napoleon was not finished yet and after an initial reverse at La Rothière in northeastern France at the beginning of February, he won five major battles in the area that same month at Champaubert, Montmirail, Château-Thierry, Vauchamps and Montereau. In March he defeated Blücher at Caronne, northeast of Paris, but was then himself defeated by the Prussians at nearby Lâon, opening the road to the capital itself and forcing Napoleon's army back to Rheims. Here Napoleon defeated the Allies in what was to be his last victory of the war. Meanwhile, the Austrians prevailed at the battles of Arcis-sur-Aube and La Fère Champenoise in Champagne and, in the very last battle of the war, Wellington defeated the French at the Battle of Toulouse on 10 April. Four days earlier Napoleon had abdicated (Wellington did not receive the news until 12 April) and, after surviving a suicide attempt, he was sent into exile on the Mediterranean island of Elba. France then voted in favour of a return of the Bourbon monarchy and the exiled brother of Louis XVI took the throne as Louis XVIII.

The Fencing Class
Gottfried Schadow, April 1814

At the Battle of Lâon, 77 miles northeast of Paris, General Blücher's Prussian forces defeated Napoleon and opened the road to the French capital. Empress Marie-Louise and the infant King of Rome left the city on 29 March and it capitulated two days later. In this German cartoon (*above*) a tiny Napoleon faces the fencing master Blücher as John Bull's naval incarnation, Jack Tar, looks on. To the left are two 'brother Germans' from the lower and upper German states and a mounted Cossack, while to the right are three anxious French military officers.

The Triumph of the Year 1813
Johann Michael Voltz, January 1814

This is one of the best known images of the Napoleonic Wars. Originally drawn as 'True Portrait of the Conqueror' by the German artist Johann Michael Voltz, it was later reproduced and adapted in seven countries and also appeared in pottery designs and other merchandise. It is even referred to in Thomas Hardy's novel of the Napoleonic Wars, *The Trumpet Major* (1882). The caricature is a parody of a popular print of Napoleon wearing the Légion d'Honneur by the Hanoverian artist Heinrich Dähling (1773-1850). Dähling's original portrait was sketched during a parade on Napoleon's triumphal visit to Berlin in October-November 1806. Voltz's 'hieroglyphic head' or 'corpse head' appeared in January 1814 and sums up Napoleon's position at the beginning of the New Year after his disastrous defeat at Leipzig (in Germany, the year 1813 was known as 'The Year of Triumph'). The German original – which allegedly sold 20,000 copies in Berlin in a single week – has the

following explanation of the drawing: Napoleon's hat is the Prussian eagle 'which has seized the great man in its claws and will not let go'; his face shows 'a few of the bodies of the 100,000 men which his lust for glory sacrificed'; the collar is 'the great stream of blood so long outpoured for his ambition'; the coat is part of the map of the dissolved Confederation of the Rhine ('at all the places indicated he lost a battle'); and the epaulet is the Hand of God about to tear apart the web 'wherein Germany was ensnared and destroy the insect [*sic*] which held the position which ought to have been occupied by the heart'. The version shown here is that published by Ackermann in London and has some additional details – the motto of the Order of the Garter (*Honi Soit Qui Mal y Pense*), 'R' (for Prince Regent) on the wrist of the hand, and rings with initials signifying Austria, Russia, Prussia and Sweden.

Shepherd and Wolf
Ivan Terebenev, 1814

Blücher the Brave Extracting the Groan of Abdication from the Corsican Bloodhound
Thomas Rowlandson, 9 April 1814

Blücher's successes over the French were much fêted as can be seen in these drawings. Rowlandson's 'Blücher the Brave' (*above*) – showing the Prussian general holding the dog Napoleon (stripped of his uniform and crown) by the scruff of his neck – is an adaptation of Terebenev's earlier Russian original (*top*) featuring Tsar Alexander I in the same role. (Note Louis XVIII being greeted by happy Frenchmen in the background.) Also by Rowlandson is 'A Friendly Visit' (*opposite top*) in which the visitor is the Devil who holds out a hangman's noose to Napoleon while the figure of Death grabs Joseph Bonaparte as he tries to escape. 'The Devil's Darling'

(*opposite bottom right*) is a re-etching by Rowlandson of a German original published at the time of the German War of Liberation against the French and shows a baby Napoleon held by a devil (note the Légion d'Honneur in its hand). By 1814 French cartoonists were also beginning to turn against their former emperor as can be seen in 'The Carnival of 1814' (*opposite bottom left*) in which Napoleon is dressed as Harlequin (pledging gold) and Cambacérès as Pulchinello (with a bowl whose contents are marked 'Conscription of 1808, 1809 etc'). Behind them stands a one-legged, one-armed man with a hospital ticket in his pocket.

A Friendly Visit
Thomas Rowlandson, 16 April 1814

The Carnival of 1814
French print, 1814

The Devil's Darling
Thomas Rowlandson, 2 March 1814

The Jay Stripped of its Borrowed Plumes
French print, 1814

Serpens Afer
French print, April 1814

These two cartoons also comment on the perceived situation of Napoleon at the beginning of 1814, though in fact the French had won a number of victories early in the year. The French drawing, 'The Jay Stripped of its Borrowed Plumes' (*top*) has Napoleon as the jay being stripped of its feathers – and the crowns of Spain, Bohemia and Poland (seen flying away) – by the eagles of (left to right) Prussia, Austria, Sweden and Russia (which is removing his crown and Légion D'Honneur medal). This is actually a French version of an earlier British print 'The Daw Stript of His Borrow'd Plumes, *vide Gay's Fables of the Daw and the Other Birds*', published on 10 November 1813. (The *Fables* of John Gay [1685-1732], best known for *The Beggar's Opera*, were published in 1738.) 'Serpens Afer' or African serpent (*above*) has Napoleon as a monstrous snake – with its coils forming the letter N (for Napoleon) – which feeds on soldiers (note the human remains and the bodies of troops in front of a burning town).

The German print 'Blowing Bubbles' (*right*) has Napoleon blowing bubbles for the amusement of his son. The bubbles are labelled (bottom to top): The Great Empire, Rome, Spain, Italy, Westphalia and Naples. The French version of Cruikshank's cartoon (*below*) has the remains of Napoleon as a spinning top being whipped by the Allies. On the ground is a leg marked 'Italy/Switzerland' and arms labelled 'Portugal/Spain' and 'France' while to the left the Prince of Orange holds up another leg marked 'Holland'. The other Allies are (left to right): Wellington, Schwartzenberg of Austria, Prince Mikhail Vorontsov of Russia (note that his whip is labelled 'knout'), Crown Prince Charles-Jean of Sweden (standing without whip), and Blücher of Prussia. Driving off in a carriage on the road behind are Empress Marie-Louise and the King of Rome while, in the sky above, Murat escapes on the tail of a demon.

Blowing Bubbles – Thus Vanish the Dreams of World Empire
German print, 1814

The Corsican Whipping-Top in Full Spin
French version of George Cruikshank print, 11 April 1814

The Representatives of Civilisation on the Way to Paris
French print, 1814

On 30 March 1814, 107,000 Allied troops faced 23,000 French at Montmartre on the outskirts of Paris and soon afterwards an armistice was signed. News of the end of the war was greeted with wild enthusiasm in the capitals of the Allied countries. In London the Prince Regent ordered a Grand Fete in the three main parks to celebrate not only the peace but also the anniversary of the Battle of the Nile (see pp.30-31) and the centenary of the British House of Hanover (George I had come to the throne of Britain in 1714). The main attraction was the re-enactment of the Battle of the Nile in a mock sea-battle (naumachia) on the Serpentine in Hyde Park.

The French print (*above*) shows Russian troops (with their loot) entering Paris, the first time since the 100 Years' War that a foreign army had entered the city. Meanwhile, the Allied view is summed up in Cruikshank's cartoon (*right*) which has a huge Cossack soldier snuffing out the tiny Napoleon candle.

Snuffing Out Boney!
George Cruikshank, 1 May 1814

British print (detail), 1814

This detail from a British print (*above*) depicts
the Hyde Park fair (complete with hot-air balloon
ascent, fireworks and naumachia in the
Serpentine) which was held on 1 August 1814.
There were also celebrations in St James's Park
and Green Park with fireworks arranged by Sir
William Congreve, inventor of the Congreve
military rocket.

The Signing of the Abdication
George Cruikshank in William Combe, *The Life of Napoleon* (1815)

A Game of Cribbage, or Boney's Last Shuffle
George Cruikshank, 6 June 1814

Peace and Plenty, or Good News for John Bull!
George Cruikshank, 24 May 1814

A Side Dish for the City of London Feast, June 18th 1814
British print, 1814

On 6 April 1814, at the palace of Fontainebleau outside Paris, Napoleon signed the formal act of abdication. Moves were then made to reinstall a Bourbon king on the throne of France. With the help of the Prince Regent, Louis XVI's younger brother – who had been in exile in England since 1807 – was chosen. Nearly 60 years old, overweight and suffering from gout he was eventually installed in the Tuileries Palace as Louis XVIII. (Louis XVI's 10-year-old son, Louis XVII, had died in captivity in France, uncrowned, in 1795.) As for Napoleon, the Allies agreed that he would be exiled as sovereign of the 18-mile-long Mediterranean island of Elba, situated between Corsica and the Tuscan coast of Italy, and which then had a population of 12,000.

In Cruikshank's 'A Game of Cribbage' (*opposite bottom left*), Napoleon plays an eight of clubs but is beaten when the Prince Regent calls '18' and lays down a king – Louis XVIII. (Note the guillotine and Cap of Liberty on the back of the tiny Napoleon's chair.) 'Peace and Plenty' (*opposite bottom right*) has the Prince Regent at the window (right) of an inn named 'The Old Constitution – New Revived by John Bull' from which he sends down food and drink to Louis XVIII (left) and John Bull. In the background Napoleon can be seen on Elba. 'A Side Dish' (*above*) refers to a banquet held at the Guildhall in London to celebrate the defeat of Napoleon. (Note Blücher's carving knife next to the trussed Napoleon.) The handbill 'Cruce Dignus' (*right*) includes a portrait of Napoleon as a strange wild beast captured for the Grand Menagerie by John Bull and the British Bulldog. He has 'the Cunning of the Fox, the Rapacity of the Wolf, the blood-thirsty Nater [*sic*] of the Hyena, the tender feelings of the Crocodile, and the Obstinacy of an Ass'. The title 'Cruce Dignus' is explained as 'an Epitaph underneath a gibbet over a Dunghill at Elba'.

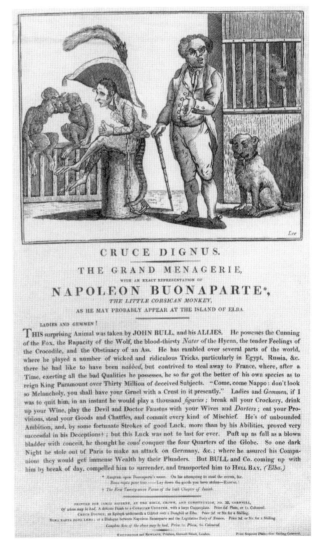

Cruce Dignus
British print, 1814

A Grand Manoeuvre!, or the Rogue's March to the Island of Elba
George Cruikshank, 13 April 1814

The Tyrant Unmasked
French print, 1814

In despair at his fall and deserted by his friends, Napoleon tried to commit suicide by taking poison at Fontainebleau on 12 April. However, when this failed he bid farewell to his Imperial Guard on the 20th and was escorted off to the Mediterranean coast. However, on his journey he was greeted with increasing hostility by the French public, notably in Provence where he was hanged in effigy and angry mobs cried 'Death to the Tyrant!' and threatened to attack him. As a result he disguised himself first as a postillion, riding in front of his own carriage, and later even wore an Austrian uniform. He arrived at Fréjus on the south coast of France on 27 April 1814. The following day he boarded a British ship, HMS *Undaunted*, and sailed to Elba.

Cruikshank's 'A Grand Manoeuvre' (*above*) has the club-footed Talleyrand getting his own back on the former French Emperor as he prods Napoleon (with a tiny King of Rome in his pocket) with an 'Allied Broom' towards the boat to Elba (note the gibbet) manned by the Devil. The French cartoon, 'The Tyrant Unmasked' (*left*), implies that the French people felt they had been misled by Napoleon who is revealed to be a tiger. This sentiment is echoed in the second French drawing (*opposite top left*) which shows a 'born again' Royalist celebrating the return of the monarchy. (Note that as he celebrates a soldier is stealing his wife and a pickpocket is taking his purse.) Meanwhile, the Esser drawing (*opposite top right*) makes fun of Napoleon as he rides off on a French cockerel, and Cruikshank (*opposite bottom*) has a Cossack dragging a chained Napoleon in a cage off to Hell/Elba.

The Perfect Royalist
French print, 1814

Napoleon Riding a Cock to Elba
W. Esser, 1814

The Elbaronian Emperor Going to Take Possession of His New Territory
George Cruikshank, 23 April 1814

The Arrival on the Island of Elba
George Cruikshank in William Combe, *The Life of Napoleon* (1815)

**The Arrival of Napoleon
on the Island of Elba**
French print, 1814

The Elba Robinson Crusoe
French print, 1814

Napoleon and his escort arrived at Portoferraio, Elba, on 4 May. Though exiled to the island – which he would rule as a sovereign principality – Napoleon was allowed by the Allies to keep his title of Emperor and to take with him 800 veterans of his Old Guard. He soon settled into his new home, the Petit Palace des Moulins, and began work organising the island's inhabitants, building roads and canals and improving the vineyards. The name of the capital was changed from Portoferraio to Cosmopoli, a new flag was designed and Napoleon received many visitors. However, he was disappointed that members of his family were not allowed to join him on Elba, as had been agreed by the Allies.

These drawings all show Napoleon's despair on Elba. The French cartoon (*above right*) – with a caption in French, German and Italian – has the former emperor carrying a broken sceptre and a copy of his book of civil law, the *Code Napoleon*. Another anonymous French cartoon (*left*) sees Napoleon as the shipwrecked mariner in Daniel Defoe's *Robinson Crusoe* (1719). Cruikshank's 'Broken Gingerbread' (*opposite top left*) alludes to Gillray's famous 'Tiddy Doll' cartoon from 1806 (see p.74) – note that the sign says 'Removed from Paris', while across the water can be seen the French rejoicing at the return of Louis XVIII. 'Little Boney Gone to Pot' (*opposite bottom*) has Napoleon sitting on a chamber pot labelled 'Imperial Throne' while a devil offers him a pistol to shoot himself (note the imperial crow nailed to the tree instead of an imperial eagle).

Broken Gingerbread
George Cruikshank, 21 August 1814

**The Sorrows of Boney,
or Meditations in the Island of Elba**
British print, 15 April 1814

Little Boney Gone to Pot
George Cruikshank, 12 May 1814

1815

WHILE THE DELEGATIONS from the four victorious Great Powers – Britain, Russia, Austria and Prussia (with Talleyrand representing France) – met at the Congress of Vienna (1814-15) to sort out new boundaries for Europe, Napoleon escaped from Elba. Landing in the south of France in March 1815 he headed north to Paris, via Grenoble, avoiding Royalist Provence. Everywhere he went he was greeted warmly and even Marshal Ney, who had promised the new French government that he would bring him back in a cage, defected to the former Emperor. By the time Napoleon reached Paris he had gathered a sizeable army and entered unopposed (Louis XVIII had fled to Belgium). The nations gathered in Vienna immediately branded him an outlaw and formed a Seventh Coalition directed not at France but at Napoleon himself. Thus began the 'Hundred Days' of Napoleonic rule. One of the first actions was the Battle of Tolentino in central Italy, in May, in which Napoleon's brother-in-law Marshal Murat, King of Naples, was defeated by Austrian forces. Napoleon's newly formed Army of the North then drove into southern Belgium in an attempt to divide the two Allied armies assembled there – under Blücher and Wellington – before they could unite with each other and the approaching armies of Austria and Russia to launch a major offensive. After taking Charleroi, Napoleon defeated Blücher's Prussian army at Ligny near Namur and marched on towards Brussels. Though another battle at Quatre Bras near Brussels was indecisive Napoleon was finally beaten by combined Allied forces under Wellington and Blücher at the Battle of Waterloo on 18 June.

After his defeat Napoleon again abdicated and headed for the port of Roquefort with the intention of sailing to the USA but, finding the harbour blockaded by the Royal Navy, changed his mind and surrendered instead to the British on 15 July, hoping to live in exile in England. However, after he had been transported across the Channel to the south coast on HMS *Bellerophon*, the British government decided to send him to the island of St Helena in the South Atlantic off the west coast of Africa. Napoleon arrived there on HMS *Northumberland* in October 1815 and died on the island on 5 May 1821.

German print, 1815

Though Napoleon had abdicated at Fontainebleau he later added that he had 'yielded nothing' and promised his supporters that he would return 'in the violet season'. On 26 February 1815, while the island's governor was away in Florence, he eluded his sleeping guard, embarked with almost 1100 troops on the French brig *L'Inconstant* and several smaller vessels, and escaped from Elba. He landed in the Golfe Juan, between Fréjus and Antibes, on 1 March 1815 – just as the violets began to bloom – and marched north the following day.

In the German print (*opposite*) Napoleon escapes his sleeping guards, tramples on his act of abdication and heads for the ship outside. The two pictures on this page relate to Napoleon's role as Papa Violet or Corporal Violet. In the pro-Napoleon print (*right*), profile portraits of Napoleon, Empress Marie-Louise and their son the King of Rome are hidden amongst the flowers. Cruikshank (*below*) makes fun of this and similar Napoleonic 'puzzle pictures' and has Napoleon growing from a dunghill. At the bottom is a 'Republican Toadstool', then an 'Imperial Sunflower', topped by a puzzle-picture bunch of violets. At the bottom left can be seen Blücher, Wellington and (behind) Tsar Alexander I rushing to destroy the plant while Louis XVIII cheers them on.

French print, 1815

The Pedigree of Corporal Violet
George Cruikshank, 9 June 1815

The Imperial Stride
French print, March 1815

Napoleon's escape came as a shock to the Peace Congress at Vienna which had been sitting for six months (it began in September 1814 and closed in June 1815). The first act of the Allies (including France) was to declare Napoleon an outlaw who was acting entirely on his own without the support of the legitimate French government. Each country pledged 150,000 troops to fight him.

'The Imperial Stride' (*left*) has Louis XVIII (centre) and the Royalist leader the Duke of Angoulême (son of King Charles X) – and his wife – looking through telescopes at the giant Napoleon striding the gap between Elba and the French mainland (two other French Royalists wear extinguishers on their heads, denoting that they will soon perish). 'The European Pantomime' (*bottom*) by Lewis Marks (fl.1814-32) features Louis XVIII (left) shaking his crutch at Napoleon (right) dressed as Harlequin who leaps across from Elba. The members of the Congress of Vienna appear in a tent in the centre, dividing up the globe, while Empress Marie-Louise and the infant King of Rome (dressed as the Pope), wave from a hilltop. The Epinal print (*opposite top*) shows Napoleon and his small army being greeted by friends in the Golfe Juan while the French Royalist cartoon (*opposite bottom*) has him riding a jackal wearing a *bonnet rouge* which is being pulled by a devil (the figure of Death follows behind).

The European Pantomime – Principal Characters: Harlequin Mr Boney, Pantaloon Louis XVIII, Columbine Maria-Louiza, Clowns etc by Congress
Lewis Marks, 1815

Epinal French print, 1815

Return from the Island of Elba
French print, 1815

141

The Firebrand
German print, 1815

Epinal French print, 1815

The Idol of the French
German print, 1815

Avoiding the Royalist heartland in the south of France, Napoleon headed through the Alps and reached Grenoble on 7 March. Everywhere he went he was greeted with enthusiasm and increasing numbers of soldiers joined his army. Even Marshal Ney, who had been sent by the French Government to capture him and had promised that he would bring him back in an iron cage, was won over and joined his former Emperor at Auxerre on 18 March. Napoleon reached Fontainebleau on 20 March where he learnt that Louis XVIII and his entourage had already fled Paris for Ghent in Belgium.

The first German cartoon 'The Firebrand' (*opposite top*) has Napoleon holding a flaming torch as his troops sack farms across France. By contrast is the Epinal print (*opposite bottom*) in which he is greeted warmly by townsfolk. The second German cartoon 'The Idol of the French' (*above*) is based on 'Hell Hounds Rallying Round the Idol of France' (April 1815) by Thomas Rowlandson and features Napoleon – with a noose around his neck and resting on a pile of severed heads – being worshipped as an idol. In both versions he is being given a crown of burning pitch by winged devils while hell-hounds dance around him. In Rowlandson's original version these are labelled with the names of Napoleon's loyal generals: Savary, Vandamme, Fouché, Davoût, Caulaincourt, Ney and Lefebvre.

The Toasts
French print, 1815

'Vive L'Empereur!'
Adolphe Willette, n.d.

Napoleon reached the Tuileries Palace in Paris on 21 March 1815 and thus began the 'Reign of a Hundred Days'. He had a mixed reception from the population but was welcomed by the army. The pro-Bonaparte 'The Toasts' (*above*) has a Parisian family toasting Napoleon as protector, revenger, vanquisher and pacifier while the drawing (*left*) by Adolphe Willette (1857-1926) – produced much later – has a one-legged veteran cheering Napoleon's return as Death grabs him by the neck.

An Eruption of Mount Vesuvius, and the Anticipated Effects of the Approaching Storm
George Cruikshank, 17 June 1815

One of the first major actions of the Hundred Days was at Tolentino in central Italy, 100 miles north of Rome. At the Battle of Tolentino (3 May 1815) Napoleon's brother-in-law Marshal Murat, King of Naples, was defeated by Austrian forces. Meanwhile, Napoleon himself began to recruit soldiers for a new Grand Army.

In Cruikshank's cartoon (*above*) Mount Vesuvius (the volcano overlooking Naples) is seen erupting and hurling Murat and his wife (Napoleon's sister Caroline) sky-high (note the loss of his crown and sceptre which are seen heading for their rightful owner, Ferdinand IV). The Bay of Naples is full of ships showing both British and French flags. Meanwhile, on the mainland of France the effects of all this can be seen, with Napoleon falling off his horse after being hit by thunderbolts emanating from the 'coming storm'. Paris is shown in flames in the background and the figures in the stormclouds are Tsar Alexander I, Frederick William III of Prussia, Louis XVIII, Blücher and Wellington. Above them, in the sun, flies the dove of peace with an olive branch in its mouth.

The Corsican and His Bloodhounds at the Window of the Tuileries Looking Over Paris
Thomas Rowlandson, 16 April 1815

Departure for the Army
French print, June 1815

Once settled in Paris, Napoleon drew up a new constitution. More than 600 delegates were then elected to the Chamber of Representatives and Napoleon himself appointed the members of the Chamber of Peers (the Senate). He also began a call to arms for 500,000 men to supplement the standing army of 200,000 left by Louis XVIII. However, though about half the National Guard subsequently enlisted, many – especially in the southern provinces – refused to join Napoleon. As a result his forces were small compared to the combined armies of all Europe and his only hope lay in attacking his enemies individually before they could concentrate their power against him.

Rowlandson's famous cartoon (*above*) has Napoleon and Marshal Ney being embraced by the Devil on the balcony of the Tuileries Palace while the figure of Death points to the mob carrying decapitated heads on pikes. An hourglass balances on the balcony rail which is itself labelled 'More Horrors' and 'Death and Destruction'. The French print (*left*) comments on the building of Napoleon's new army. In it the Emperor rides a skeleton horse on whose tail sits a tattered French eagle. In one hand Napoleon holds a bundle of thunderbolts while in the other is a document which reads: 'I am going to fight my enemies!! Appeal for 500,000 men.' Meanwhile, Cruikshank (*opposite*) criticises the new constitution and the Code Napoleon. (Note the sails of the windmill which imply the fickleness of the French: 'Long Live the King', 'Long Live the Emperor', 'Long Live the Republic' and 'Long Live the Devil'.)

The Genius of France Expounding Her Laws to the Sublime People
George Cruikshank, 4 April 1815

The New Order
Heinrich Kley, n.d.

Ignoring for the moment the slow-moving armies of Russia and Austria, Napoleon decided to strike first at King Frederick William III's Prussian army stationed outside Ligny near Namur in southern Belgium before it could unite with the Duke of Wellington's Anglo-Dutch (and Hanoverian) force assembling near Brussels. He thus led his newly formed Army of the North across the River Sambre into Belgium on 14 June and took Charleroi on the road to Brussels. Napoleon then defeated the Prussians under Field Marshal Gebhard von Blücher at the Battle of Ligny (16 June). French casualties were 11,500 but the Prussians lost 23,000 (including 12,000 deserters) and Blücher himself was injured. News of Napoleon's crossing the Sambre and taking Charleroi caught the Allies on the hop, Wellington (and many of the British and Dutch commanders) famously receiving the information while attending the Duchess of Richmond's lavish ball in Brussels.

Allegorical Subject
French print, 1815

The two cartoons on the opposite page show the figure of Death leading Napoleon into a hopeless new war. The Royalist French drawing, 'Allegorical Subject' (*opposite bottom*), has Death (note the crown of violets) playing a violin and dancing a jig while leading a mad-looking Napoleon (trampling over treaties) and three harpies – Discord (a gorgon), War and Poverty/Misery. The German cartoon by Schadow (*right*) has Napoleon, holding a sword and firebrand, leaping from his war chariot (drawn by vicious dogs) across the River Sambre which borders France and Belgium. John Bull watches from a boat while relaxed Prussian soldiers prepare to repel his advances, undisturbed by the sound of Glory's trumpet. William Heath, meanwhile (*below*), depicts the moment during the ball in Brussels when Wellington receives the shock news of the defeat of Blücher at Ligny (note the upturned chair and swooning lady at the left).

The Leap Across the Sambre
Gottfried Schadow, 1815

The Duchess of Richmond's Ball, or Intelligence of the Battle of Ligny
William Heath in *Wellington's Victories* (1818)

The Sacrifice of Napoleon Bonaparte (18 June 1815)
French print, June 1815

Report of the Courier in the Chamber of Peers
Gottfried Schadow, 1815

While Napoleon was fighting Blücher at Ligny a separate force of 25,000 French troops under Marshal Ney attacked an Anglo-Dutch detachment of 37,000 under Wellington outside the Belgian village of Quatre Bras, 20 miles southeast of Brussels. Though the Battle of Quatre Bras (16 June 1815) was indecisive (both sides lost about 4000 troops) it slowed the French advance and allowed Wellington to regroup and concentrate his main force of 100,000 troops at his pre-planned defensive position at Mont St Jean four miles south of the village of Waterloo and 12 miles from Brussels. Napoleon was finally beaten at the Battle of Waterloo on 18 June 1815 when Blücher's force of 125,000 Prussians arrived to reinforce Wellington's army. (It was named Waterloo as Wellington had set up his headquarters in the village, but to the French it is known as the Battle of Mont St Jean and to the Germans as the Battle of La Belle Alliance – the name of an inn two miles from Mont St Jean which was Napoleon's headquarters and at which Wellington and Blücher met after the battle.) French casualties were 44,000 while the Allies lost 23,000.

In the French cartoon (*top*) Death (again playing a fiddle) sits on the back of Napoleon's horse. As Bonaparte points to lines of French soldiers going into battle he says: 'I sacrifice all this to you as well.' Death replies: '*You* will come to this end too.' Schadow's German cartoon (*bottom*) shows a messenger (right) announcing the French disaster at Waterloo to Napoleon's supporters in the Chamber of Peers in Paris. He points out of the window to the battlefield where Glory in her chariot drawn by vicious dogs has just been shot and Napoleon can be seen escaping (having lost his hat). Inside, all the members appear shocked and Marianne has completely fainted (a devilish doctor feels her pulse).

In the cartoon by Marks (*below*), Napoleon is shown being boiled in a pot above a fire labelled 'Waterloo' while Blücher (left) and Wellington look on. 'Portrait of a Noble Duke' (*right*) – in a similar technique employed in the earlier 'corpse-head' portrait of Napoleon by Voltz (see p.125) – has Wellington's head made entirely of military paraphernalia. His ear is a drum, his nose is a field tent (with a sentry-box below), his chin is a stone fortress wall with cannon for teeth, his jawbone is a sabre, he has cannons for eyes and bayonets for eyelashes, flags cover his cheek and forehead – the latter with the titles of his most famous victories at Vittoria, Salamanca (both from the Peninsular War) and Waterloo – and his hair is made of laurel leaves (the classical symbol of victory). Below the picture is the quotation: '"I should think this head possest some talent for Military affairs" *Phrenological Lecture*.'

Portrait of a Noble Duke
William Heath, 1829

Boney in a Stew!!
Lewis Marks, July 1815

The Last Brew
French version of George Cruikshank print, 20 June 1815

La Belle Alliance – Sweeping France Clean
Johann Michael Voltz, 1815

The Big Drum of Europe
French print, 1815

There were many cartoons on Napoleon's defeat at Waterloo, including – for the first time – a great many French ones against the nation's former leader. In 'The Last Brew' (*opposite top*) – a French version of a Cruikshank original – Blücher (left) and Wellington boil up the French army for the last time, assisted by a three-headed monster representing the other main Allies – Russia, Austria and Sweden. Voltz, meanwhile (*opposite bottom*), has gigantic British and Prussian soldiers sweeping France clean of the tiny Napoleon and his supporters, some of whom are seen drowning in the English Channel off Rochefort. 'The Big Drum' (*above*) is a French version of an earlier anonymous British original ('Drumming Out of the French Army', June 1814) in which a British drum-major is seen beating a big drum in the form of Napoleon.

This is What Comes of Having Too Much Heart
French print, July 1815

Napoleon abdicated four days after his defeat at Waterloo and left Paris in disguise, heading for the Channel port of Roquefort. His intention was to sail from there to the USA, knowing he would be executed by the Royalists if he stayed in France. However, finding the harbour blockaded by the Royal Navy, he changed his mind and surrendered instead to the British on 15 July, hoping to live in exile in England like his brother Lucien (see p.74). He was then transported across the Channel to the south coast on HMS *Bellerophon* and after mooring in Torbay in Devon (24 July) wrote a personal letter to the Prince Regent formally requesting permission to stay in Britain. However, to his dismay the Prince Regent did not reply directly and instead the Government made a decision to send him to the opposite side of the earth and exile him on the British South Atlantic island of St Helena. After sailing to Plymouth, Napoleon was transferred to HMS *Northumberland* which set off for St Helena on 11 August, accompanied by several other warships.

The *Ne Plus Ultra* of Cannibalism
French print, 1815

In the first French cartoon (*opposite top*), Napoleon is seen writing, with his hand on his heart, 'Napoleon surrenders but does not die' – the reverse of what he commanded his Imperial Guard to do on the field of Waterloo ('The Guard dies but it does not surrender'). He is shown writing this on the base of the Victory Column in the Place Vendôme, Paris – which he erected after the French victory at Austerlitz and which is shown guarded by foreign soldiers – above laurel wreaths marking the battles from which he has escaped like a hare (drawn below). The words in the wreaths are: 'He has fled from Egypt, Spain, Moscow, Leipzig and Mont St Jean [Waterloo].' The very detailed *'Ne Plus Ultra* of Cannibalism' (*opposite bottom*) has Napoleon seated on a leopard above a pile of corpses including the Duc d'Enghien while behind him Moscow burns and a river of blood flows in the foreground. The third French drawing (*right*) shows Napoleon finally achieving his ambition of landing in England, though ironically it is not as the leader of a French invasion fleet but in chains as a prisoner of the British. The final French cartoon (*below*) has Napoleon leaping from HMS *Bellerophon* to HMS *Northumberland* prior to his departure to St Helena and saying 'Leave me, Bertrand.' Below him, holding a French eagle and his imperial crown, is his trusted friend Grand Marshal Bertrand (who had been with him on Elba).

Bonaparte Finally Achieves his Project of Landing in England
French print, 1815

The Leap from *Bellerophon*
French print, 1815

Boney's Meditations on the Island of St Helena, or The Devil Addressing the Sun – *Paradise Lost*, **Book IV**
George Cruikshank, 1815

The Prometheus of St Helena
French print, 1815

After a 70-day voyage, Napoleon arrived at the mountainous volcanic island of St Helena in the South Atlantic, 1200 miles off the west coast of Africa, on 17 October 1815. An isolated supply-station for British merchant ships, it was only 47 square miles in area (half the size of Elba) and had a population of about 4000. It was also known to be infested with rats. Napoleon was accompanied to St Helena by three of his most loyal former generals – Grand Marshal Bertrand, De Montholon and Gourgaud – and the Comte de Las Cases, a close confidant.

Cruikshank's drawing (*left*) is an adaptation of Gillray's earlier 'Gloria Mundi, or the Devil Addressing the Sun' (1784) – with Fox in the place of Napoleon – and alludes to Satan's soliloquy after his fall in Book IV of John Milton's epic poem *Paradise Lost* (1667). Napoleon – with devilish cloven hoofs, tattered wings and horns – stands on St Helena and curses the Prince Regent, depicted as the Sun. The radiating sunbeams have the names of the Allied leaders: Alexander I (of Russia), Frederick William III (of Prussia), Francis I (of Austria), William I of Orange (Holland), Wellington, Blücher, Hill (Wellington's second-in-command), Beresford and Anglesey (commander of cavalry at Waterloo). The French cartoon (*below*) has Napoleon chained to the mountains of St Helena like Prometheus of Greek mythology who, having stolen fire, was condemned by Zeus to be chained to a rock and have an eagle continuously pecking at his liver. In this version a vulture labelled 'Rage' pecks at Napoleon's heart. At his feet is a candlestick marked 'Torch of Prometheus' but the candle's flame – Glory – has been put out for ever by an extinguisher marked 'Waterloo'. In the second French cartoon (*opposite top*) Napoleon, dressed in French imperial robes – but with the nose of Pulchinello (Punch) from the Italian Commedia dell'Arte – swears in his military council of rats, two of whose leaders take the oath. The third French print (*opposite bottom left*) has a weeping Napoleon sitting on a rock on the rat-infested island and smoking a pipe. In the final drawing (*opposite bottom right*), the artist puns on the French words *pécheur* (sinner) and *pêcheur* (angler). Napoleon, the great sinner/angler, is thus shown standing on St Helena, fishing bodies out of the sea and catching the Duc d'Enghien whom he had executed without cause in 1804 (see p.62).

French print, 1815

French print, 1815

La Grand Pécheur
French print, 21 July 1815

Memorable Event of 1821
French print, 1821

Napoleon died in Longwood House, his residence on St Helena, on 5 May 1821. He was buried nearby in the Geranium Valley but in 1840 his body was removed and brought to Paris to be reinterred in a lavish state ceremony in Les Invalides in December that year. The French pro-Napoleon cartoon (*above*) was published (in French) in London at the time of his death and has Glory attacking anti-Bonaparte figures who, like vultures or jackals, are eating his corpse. Cruikshank's proposed monument to Napoleon (*right*) – his last drawing to feature Bonaparte – was published on the occasion of the return of his body to France in 1840. In it the skeleton of Napoleon appears in military uniform standing on top of a pyramid of skulls, flanked by French flags. On the left the tricolour is surmounted by a *bonnet rouge* of the French Revolution and on the right by a gilded Imperial Eagle from a Napoleonic military standard.

Monument to Napoleon!
George Cruikshank, 1840

INDEX